Conscious Grieving

A Transformative
Approach to
Healing from Loss

Claire Bidwell Smith, LCPC

WORKMAN PUBLISHING · NEW YORK

To all of my clients who have trusted me with your stories of loss.
You have taught me more about life and love than I ever could
have imagined and I am forever grateful.

Workman
Workman Publishing
Hachette Book Group, Inc.
1290 Avenue of the Americas
New York, NY 10104
workman.com

Workman is an imprint of Workman Publishing,
a division of Hachette Book Group, Inc.
The Workman name and logo are registered trademarks
of Hachette Book Group, Inc.

Design by Janet Vicario
Image credits: © Can Stock Photo / wertaw: interior icon, round sand dollar,
© Can Stock Photo / happyroman: cover and interior icon, conch

The publisher is not responsible for websites (or their content)
that are not owned by the publisher.

Workman books may be purchased in bulk for business, educational, or
promotional use. For information, please contact your local bookseller
or the Hachette Book Group Special Markets Department
at special.markets@hbgusa.com.

Library of Congress Cataloging-in-Publication Data is available.

ISBN: 978-1-5235-2028-2

First Edition March 2024

Printed in the USA on responsibly sourced paper.

10 9 8 7 6 5 4 3 2 1

Contents

Introduction

Loss is something that happens to us. But how we choose to grieve is up to us.

I believe that we innately know how to grieve and that it's a birthright we must reclaim. As our culture has evolved over the centuries, much has changed about our approach to death. Dying has become increasingly medicalized, hidden from sight and avoided at all costs, while our pursuit of youth and longevity has risen dramatically. The result is a distance around community, ritual, and intention surrounding end of life and grief.

Yet death remains inevitable. As such, so does grief. The difference is that we have agency over the latter. We all have the capacity to survive loss, and we also have the ability to transform through grief. To do so requires being conscious to the experience.

When we lose someone we love, the grief we experience can feel like something that is happening to us. it's normal to feel out of control and overwhelmed. But true healing from loss actually begins when you engage with your grief, open yourself up to it, learn how to integrate it into your life, and eventually let it transform you.

You are here because you are in pain. You are seeking reassurance and safety. You are seeking guidance for this thing that has happened to you. You are hurting and you are afraid. It's okay to feel all of those things and more. And it's okay to be grieving.

Grief is the natural human response to losing someone or something. You have grieved before, even if it wasn't like this. Grief and loss have always been here. And it's time to welcome them in.

Our culture tends to shy away from addressing loss, which results in a message to those who are grieving that they need to move through their grief quickly and privately. Or grief is treated as an affliction, as

Entering into grief encompasses the initial experiences and feelings we encounter at the start of the grief journey. Denial, overwhelm, and anxiety stemming from the immediate physical, emotional, and practical life changes that occur after loss are all common characteristics of this period. Allowing for a gentle awareness of these emotions will enable you to begin grieving consciously. In this section you will learn about grief, what's normal and okay, and about what you can expect from the people around you, as well as how to take care of yourself and stay present as you start out on this path.

Engaging with grief explores the more complicated aspects of grief that we encounter once we have moved past the initial phases of loss. Guilt, depression, anger, and shame all have their place here. As does coping with multiple losses, holidays and anniversaries, family and community, and what to expect in the first year of a loss. Often our instinct is to run and avoid so many of these complicated aspects, but we will explore how staying present and in tune with your needs is more beneficial to the process.

Surrendering to grief focuses on changes to your identity and on who you are becoming in the face of loss. When we stop resisting change and surrender, the doors of spirituality, self-compassion, and resilience open. This section explores how to support yourself as you undergo these changes to your world and how to consciously allow for so much unexpected change.

Transforming through grief presents the idea that there is an opportunity within your experience to build a meaningful life. Transformation requires the use of ritual, honor, hope, humility, and grace. While sometimes these may feel elusive, there are ways we can learn to carry our grief consciously so that we may continue to grow, heal, and thrive.

Throughout each section you will notice a repetition of themes such as forgiveness and self-compassion, as well as repeated topics like family dynamics, identity shifts, and markers of time. That is because these themes and inflection points are ones that we come back to in many different iterations throughout the grief process. And with the progression of time, we must continue to orient ourselves by seeking new understanding from these themes.

You will also notice that there are invitations for reflection at the end of every chapter. Keeping a journal handy while you read this book would be a helpful accompaniment to your quest for healing. For each reflection, you may wish to think for a while or go straight into journaling a response. Being able to go back and reflect on what you've written will help you gain a better insight into your newfound understandings of yourself and your grief.

While there are no right or wrong ways to grieve, there are ways to engage with grief that can better help us along this painful journey. To grieve consciously invites the possibility for true healing and transformation. Only you know what your experience of loss entails and what you require to survive and to heal. And although I intimately understand loss both personally and professionally, there will always be more to learn and more to impart. While I have tried to cover and address anything and everything you might be experiencing, if something is missing for you from these pages, do not let that invalidate your experience. Take what resonates here; discard what doesn't fit. Give yourself permission to come back to this book many times along your journey—you will find something new each time.

PART ONE

Entering into Grief

Welcome to grief. It's not a place you've ever wished to dwell, yet here you are. You may still be in disbelief that you are here. That's okay. You may still be trying to find ways to go back to who you were before. That's okay too. You likely feel lost and overwhelmed. This isn't something you asked for, and it's probably more than you bargained for. But you don't have to do anything more than what you're doing. Just breathe. Just be here. Allow yourself to *enter* into your grief.

An Invitation

Someone you love is gone. And you are holding this book because you don't know what else to do. That's okay. You don't have to know what to do. You don't have to be good at this. You don't even have to *want* to do this. All you have to do is keep breathing.

Just be here.

I know that's hard when the person you love isn't. It may even feel impossible in certain moments. But grief is something all of us innately know how to do. It's not something you can prepare for or need to feel ready for. It is simply grief.

In the beginning, grief is a conflicting, amorphous mess of an experience. One minute you're fine. The next, you're on the floor heaving. That's okay. In fact, it's normal. And one day, a ways out from now, you may even feel a strange gratitude for who you have become through grief.

But here's the thing to know about grief: It's not an affliction. It's not an ailment. It's not something you need to get over or rush through.

Grief is part of the very real experience of being human. Grief is part of our lives all the time. You've grieved before, even if it didn't feel quite like this. And you'll grieve again. We all will.

Grief is a natural part of our lives. And the process of grieving is integral to our experience of moving through the world.

At its core, grief is about loss. And loss is about change. And change is never easy. Losing someone we love changes everything. It changes our identity. It changes our relationships. It changes the way we see the world. Loss changes the future. And sometimes even the past.

And although this kind of change is sometimes unbearable, the only way to move through it is to lean into it. In this book, I'm going to do just that. Lean into the anguish. Lean into all the ways in which your world is changing.

I know it might seem scary, like the ground might open up and swallow you whole. Like you may never stop crying. But you will not fall through the floor. And you will eventually stop crying.

Trust me, the alternative is much harder. All that aching, blinding pain you feel is not going to simply disappear if you run from it or ignore it. It will just be there waiting for you, and in the meantime it will have spilled out anyway, in all kinds of other agonizing ways that are immeasurably disrupting your life.

Let me say it again: Grief isn't something to get over. It's not something you can ignore or stifle or put a Band-Aid on. It's not going anywhere until it's had its way with you. But that doesn't have to be a bad thing. It's certainly not going to hurt any more than it already does.

Grieving is a natural process. It's not something to rush or tidy up. Grief is not going to adhere to any timelines or formulas. Grief is a human response to losing someone or something that mattered deeply to you. When you think about it that way, wouldn't it be weird if you *weren't* grieving?

But grief isn't always easy, I know. It's messy and mercurial, and it doesn't follow instructions.

That's because losing someone we love is wildly painful. More so than we could ever have imagined. We want the pain to go away. We want our person back. We want the world to stand still. We want to be held. We want to be left alone. We are scared. We are wounded animals lashing out at anyone and anything that approaches. We worry that we will never be the same again.

And we won't.

But here's the thing: You don't have to do anything except open up to your experience.

The easiest way to do that is to invite your grief in. Pull up a chair for it even. Maybe make it some tea. Get yourself a cozy blanket and curl up so you can listen to what your grief has to say.

Some of what your grief has to say will be unimaginably hard to hear—reflections of yourself and your person that might be painful to review. And choices you've made that grief will hold a mirror up to.

But keep looking in that mirror. Keep listening. Grief is also here to show you what matters. The reflection you see might also contain a lot of love, a lot of joy, and a lot of what means the most to you in this world. Maybe you've never seen those things as clearly as grief will show you.

Those things in the mirror? They aren't gone. You're just going to develop a new way of holding them. And grief is here to help you do just that.

If only you'll let it.

So, start here. Just let yourself grieve. Let yourself open up. Invite your grief in and see what it has to teach you. If that still feels impossible, I want you to imagine clenching your fist as tightly as you can, until your knuckles turn white. That's what you're doing when you're trying to resist your grief.

Now imagine opening your palm. Relax your hand. Let your fingers rest and curl as they want. That's you inviting your grief in. You don't have to do anything except surrender to the process.

And I get that's a big ask. Surrender can be scary. We spend most of our lives trying to feel like we are in control. Why would we want to surrender to all this pain?

Because the only way out is through.

The more you resist it, the more you clench your fist, the rougher it's going to be.

I have a friend who once told me that she awoke each day asking what the surprise would be. And by surprise she meant what would be the unexpected thing that would throw a wrench in her plans? The thing she hadn't allowed room for. The thing that might bring unwanted change.

But because she went into each day with the awareness that there would be *something* that she hadn't planned for, she found that she wasn't all that resistant to it when it showed up—a flat tire, an emergency phone call, an irritating interruption—instead, she found herself open to the challenge that each one of these things brought forth.

Try thinking of your grief in this way. Acknowledge the unexpectedness of it. The untidiness of it. And each time it arises—each time a new wave of grief knocks you to the floor or prompts you to move in an unfamiliar direction—surrender to it, go with it, lean into it, and let it show you the way through.

Grief is your love, your anger, your fear, and your desperate desire to have your person still here with you. Grief is even the way you will find your way back to them. It won't be the same as before. But grief will show you all the ways in which you never have to let go of them.

So, open yourself up. Invite the grief in and let it show you the way forward.

Reflection
Can you give yourself permission to grieve in a way you haven't yet?

Meet Yourself Where You Are

Your loss might have happened last week. Or maybe you lost someone many years ago. Both are important. Both are okay. More than okay. There is no time stamp on how long you get to grieve. There is no limit on how long you take to explore your grief. You may be in the initial days or weeks of a loss, desperate to find a balm to the pain you are experiencing. Or perhaps you are years out from your loss but woke up one day recently knowing that you have been avoiding your ability to engage and examine your grief in ways that will serve you. My point is, the opportunity to grieve consciously is the same, whether your loss is new or old.

If you are coming to these pages newly in the throes of grief, you are likely reeling. You are searching for something to hold onto and some way to understand what is happening. You might be feeling overwhelming anguish and sadness, even desperation and terror. And perhaps anger, fear, and guilt as well. You want to know how long this will go on for and how you will get through it. You are seeking bearings, a map, tools, strength, hope, and understanding.

If you are coming to this book with a loss that you have been carrying for some time, you might be searching for answers as to why it still feels so hard, why you feel stuck, or why your person's death continues to affect you the way it does. Perhaps you are searching for ways to stop cycling through emotions like anger and guilt and anxiety. Perhaps you are still looking for a way to be in the world without them. Perhaps you are only now in a place in which you feel able to engage consciously with your grief. Or perhaps you have grieved, but something in your life has changed and you need to grieve some more.

For those of you who are in the beginning of a loss, you may feel some fear, dread, or anxiety each time you allow yourself to think about the journey ahead. And knowing that there are others who may be coming to these pages years past where you are now might feel overwhelming, like you'll never truly get out of this place you're in. It's hard to imagine all the change that is to come and all the ways you will learn to live with your loss. Maybe for now, just take comfort in knowing that you do not have to get over your loss. Take heart that although the pain doesn't go away, it does become more bearable.

For those of you who are living with older losses, take time to reflect on the various passages. You are here for a reason. There is more grieving to do. As you read, acknowledge the pieces that you have already moved through and take time to appreciate the ways you have changed and grown. Watch for places in your grief that you may have skipped over—the parts that once felt too difficult but now feel manageable. Above all, as you read, have compassion for the person you have become since your loss, and allow room for hope about the person you are yet to become.

With grief comes growth, but we all grow at different rates.

Reflection
Create a timeline of your grief that spans your life thus far— include losses such as moves, friendship breaks, and deaths, including pets.

A Note for Those
with Complicated Relationships

Humans are complex creatures, and we often have complicated relationships. The people we lose are not always perfect. Sometimes they did not treat us well, and sometimes we did not have positive relationships with them. That doesn't mean you don't get to grieve when they are gone. No matter what your relationship was with the person you lost, your grief is real and valid.

Perhaps your person was lovely and loving, and yet you have complicated feelings about them.

Perhaps the person you lost was difficult, and you are experiencing relief or comfort in their death.

Perhaps your person caused you immense pain and hurt, and you are confused by everything you feel now that they are gone.

Perhaps you were the hurtful one, and now you are swimming in a sea of guilt and regret about how things ended.

Perhaps you had a broken relationship and had not seen your person for long time before they died.

Perhaps your person was abusive or toxic, and now that they are gone you feel relieved.

Perhaps your person suffered greatly in life, and you think that things might be easier now that they are gone.

Perhaps you are angry at the person who is gone, and you are afraid to admit that.

Perhaps others did not think highly of your person, but you still love and miss them and are afraid to share your feelings.

Grief is not just for people who had caring and supportive relationships. Grief can be felt for all kinds of relationships, even the most difficult ones. We can grieve for the very people who hurt us the most.

As you read these pages, try not to judge your grief.

It's okay to feel anger. It's okay to feel relief. It's okay to feel despair. It's okay to yearn to have someone back even though they were not a good person in your life. It's okay to feel happy. It's okay to feel regret and sadness and fury. And it's okay to feel all of it at the same time.

What's important to understand is that when we are grieving someone with whom we had a complicated relationship, there are additional layers of grief to face and resolve. We may have to process additional depths of pain and anger or guilt and resentment in ways that others may not have to. Be patient. Be kind with yourself. Let it be okay that you are feeling everything that you are feeling. Seek grace and fortitude as you make your way.

You deserve to grieve no matter who you lost.

Reflection
Write a letter to yourself, giving yourself permission to grieve this complicated relationship.

You Will Never Be the Same

You already feel a sense of before and after.

For some of us, there is relief in knowing this. We don't want anything to go on as it was. Nothing should ever be the same without this person in the world. And yet for some of us, there is additional grief when we lose the person we ourselves were before they were gone.

> "The reality is that you will grieve forever. You will not
> 'get over' the loss of a loved one; you will learn to live
> with it. You will heal and you will rebuild yourself around
> the loss you have suffered. You will be whole again, but
> you will never be the same. Nor should you be the same
> nor would you want to."
>
> —Elisabeth Kubler-Ross

But no matter if you wish to be the same or not, it is important to acknowledge this new version of yourself, even if it is strange and unfamiliar. The world, too, probably feels strange and unfamiliar now that your person is gone. The newness of everything is indisputable and immutable. It is disconcerting and frightening.

Remember that at its core, loss is about change. And you have coped with change before. Give yourself time to adjust to the newness of it all. Let yourself grieve what is slipping away. Let yourself be open and curious about what is emerging in its place.

If it helps, you can think of it as though you have been transported to a foreign land. The terrain is unfamiliar, the language is foreign, the customs are different, and the expectations are new. But just like when you travel somewhere you've never been, there are pieces of yourself that stay the same. Your core values and principles may stay intact.

Your talents and unique skills may still be in play. And your ability to love and live may stay unwavering.

Sometimes in grief, nothing changes on the outside—you are still in the same body, the same house, the same town. And sometimes everything changes externally—your location and landscape and your latitude have shifted. The point is that some of the changes might be obvious and others not so much, although you feel them all the same. Let yourself acknowledge when the changes feel welcome, and grieve for the ones uninvited.

Missing who you were before is normal. Feeling resistant to the new version of yourself happens too.

Give yourself time, more than you think. Show yourself compassion. Treat yourself as you would someone who was new to your town, workplace, or school. Give yourself a minute to learn the streets and the social norms. Forgive your anger and frustration when you get lost more than once.

Remind yourself that you didn't ask to be this new person in this new place. Your person being gone is something that happened to you. But you get to choose what happens next. You get to decide how to treat this emerging self. The more patience and love you can extend to yourself along the way, the sooner you will feel at home within yourself again.

Reflection

Write a letter to your new self about times you've faced reinvention before. What saw you through the dismantling of your old self and the invention of your new self? What strengths did you utilize? Where did you find support? Are there parts of that experience that can apply now?

What Is Grief?

In order to grieve consciously, we must get to know grief. But what is grief?

At its most simplistic, grief is the emotional, physical, and cognitive response to losing someone or something important to us.

We can grieve for many things. Yes, people. But pets too, jobs, moves, relationships, even ideas we had about ourselves or the way we thought life was going to go. When something ends or is no longer here, we experience a multitude of feelings.

Grief is with us all through our lifetimes. You have probably grieved even when you didn't know you were grieving. As a child you grieved for toys lost, friendships that fell apart, teams you didn't make, teachers you didn't get, teachers you did get but had to say goodbye to, summers gone by, holidays past, childhood, adolescence, innocence, and more.

As an adult you have grieved changes in the world, as well as changes to your body and your family. You have grieved the end of friendships and lovers, and marriages, and your own children aging. You have grieved public figures and presidential elections, wars in countries you've never been to, and shifts within your own community. You have grieved moves and careers and financial status, and you have grieved other changes that only you can name.

And with each thing lost, there have been moments of pause, moments of sadness and pain, of reflection and remorse, and a yearning you couldn't quite explain.

That was grief. *This* is grief.

Grief contains multiple dimensions, and grief resides in many places. Grief cannot be contained and limited to one single place. Rather it manifests within the physical, cognitive, behavioral, social, cultural, spiritual, and philosophical realms of our existence. And while the culture around you may try to put limits around what your grief is and isn't, just know: If you feel grief, then you are grieving.

The thing about grief is that it is amorphous and unwieldy. The true definition of grief is an elusive one because it is different for everyone. We seek formulas and equations that will explain the way we feel when we experience loss, but there is not a one-size-fits-all answer.

But grief is also not entirely mysterious. Yes, it's true that your loss is unique and your process individual, but there are practical ways to engage with grief. There are concrete tools that help. There will be moments of clarity and direction.

I lay out those paths and strategies in the pages ahead, but for now what's important is that you begin by giving yourself permission to grieve in the first place.

So right now, take a deep breath and step back from any judgment you are carrying about your grief. Just allow it to be what it is right in this very moment.

Now take another deep breath and release any pressure you feel from others about how you should be grieving. Only you know what your grief feels like.

Let yourself consider what it might be like if you stopped trying to grieve a certain way.

Allow yourself more time.

Stop resisting all the changes.

Invite yourself to be curious about your grief.

Reflection
What did you think about grief before this loss? How is this one different? What do you know now that you didn't before?

Types of Grief

Although grief is grief, there are also many different types of grief. You may recognize pieces of your experience within some or many.

ANTICIPATORY GRIEF

Anticipatory grief is everything we feel when we know we are facing loss. We might be expecting to lose a person, a pet, a house, a job, a marriage, or even a part of our bodies. When we are facing this loss, we cannot help but anticipate everything that will come with it—all the pain, sorrow, anger, fear, and life changes. Anxiety is often a companion to this anticipation as we face the uncertainty of when we will experience the loss and what it will feel like.

COMPLICATED GRIEF

Complicated grief is defined as an extended process of grieving with persistent and intense emotions that are impacting our ability to live our life. Complicated grief occurs when we experience traumatic loss, had a complex relationship with someone we lost, or when our environments or circumstances exacerbate our ability to cope. In some ways, all grief is complicated, but some of us have more layers to work through than others.

AMBIGUOUS GRIEF

Ambiguous grief results from loss that lacks closure, information, and resolution. It's the kind of grief that we feel with divorce, breakups, grief for biological parents we never knew, and also estrangement. We can feel this grief when the person we are grieving is still here, but we are disconnected from them in some way. This grief feels ambiguous because the relationship still has future potential.

DISENFRANCHISED GRIEF

Disenfranchised grief is the grief that is not readily recognized or acknowledged by those around us. Disenfranchised grief emerges in cases of pregnancy loss, infertility, racism, and other less talked about losses like retirement, pet loss, moving, and empty nesting. When your experience is minimized and your grief is not recognized, we can feel lost, empty, angry, and unsure of ourselves.

COLLECTIVE GRIEF

This is the grief we share with others when we grieve for the world at large in times of crisis and strife, as well as for public figures, celebrities, and victims of natural disasters. This grief is very real and can be powerful, but sharing our grief in this collective way can be both challenging and comforting.

Reflection
Write about a time you have experienced each of these kinds of grief.

What Grief Isn't

Sometimes the best way to define grief is to examine what it isn't.

Grief is not an illness.

Grief is not an affliction.

Grief is not a prison sentence.

Grief isn't the same for everyone.

Grief isn't over when people stop asking about your loss.

Grief is not formulaic.

Grief isn't something you get over after a few weeks.

Grief isn't neat and tidy.

Grief is not just for when we lose good things and loving relationships.

Grief isn't a universal set of feelings.

Grief isn't just for big things or big relationships.

Grief is not predictable.

Grief isn't one-dimensional.

Grief does not exist in a vacuum.

Grief isn't something you should be prepared for.

Grief is not something most people know how to talk about.

Grief isn't something you're supposed to be good at.

Grief is not just one emotion.

Grief isn't something you can compare.

Reflection
Make your own list of what grief isn't.

It's Okay—This Is Normal

While it's true that we experience grief throughout our lifetimes **in many different ways,** some grief is so big that it feels wholly unfamiliar. When this happens you might question your experience. You may doubt your response. You may need reassurance.

It's okay to feel scared.

It's normal to fantasize about what it would be like to have your person back, even any version of them.

It's okay to be angry.

It's normal to feel numb.

It's okay not to cry.

It's normal to feel like you can't stop crying.

It's okay for you to want this to all go away.

It's normal to feel forgetful.

It's okay to grieve differently from people who lost the same person you did.

It's normal to feel more than one emotion at the same time, even conflicting ones.

It's okay to want to be around people.

It's normal to want to be alone.

It's okay to laugh.

It's normal to want the world to stop.

It's okay to want to have fun.

It's normal to not feel like yourself.

It's okay to wonder if you will ever see them again.

It's normal to worry that you might forget your person.

It's okay to question your beliefs.

It's normal to need to take time off work.

It's okay to ask for help.

It's normal to feel irritable.

It's okay to feel vulnerable.

It's normal to feel tired.

It's okay to feel overwhelmed.

It's normal to feel jealous.

It's okay to feel resentful.

It's normal to feel remorseful.

It's okay to feel relief.

It's normal to worry about the future.

It's okay to talk to your person, even though they're not here anymore.

It's normal to worry about more loss.

It's okay to replay memories or images.

It's normal to feel alone.

It's okay to cling to objects and places that are connected to your person.

It's normal to avoid things and places that are connected to your person.

It's okay to grieve longer than you thought you would.

It's normal to grieve longer than other people thought you would.

It's okay to want to be around people who understand your grief.

It's normal to avoid people who don't get what you're going through.

It's okay to wonder if you're okay.

It's normal to think you might never be okay.

It's okay to hope that you will be okay.

Reflection
Make a list of any of the feelings you're unsure of. What would you tell a friend who was feeling these things?

When You Fall Apart

It's okay to fall apart. In fact, it's more than okay.

Most of us have been taught that falling apart is not acceptable. You may worry that you can't afford to fall apart, or that people will judge you if you fall apart, or you may worry that if you fall apart you may never recover. But the truth is that falling apart is actually how we come back together.

Falling apart can look like many things. For some of us it looks like breaking down in public places. For others it looks like staying in bed all day. And for still others, falling apart is hard to see from the outside.

And while it may feel like you can't let yourself fall apart, or like you can't afford to not function as usual, it's important to remember that grief often requires a departure from your usual way of being in the world. Conscious grieving almost always requires a shift in priorities. The true work of grief demands that we make time and space for it, even if that means making time to cry or taking extra time to rest.

Letting yourself fall apart means surrendering to the emotions of grief, giving yourself the release your body and soul need, and allowing space and time for processing and reflection. All of these are precisely what will set the scene for the rebuilding and rebirth that must begin to take place.

Reflection
What do you need in order to feel safe enough to fall apart?

What Grief Feels Like

While only you know what it's like to be going through this loss, you still might be questioning some of what you are feeling. The swing of emotions; the hows, whys, and what-ifs that spin through your mind; the life changes—all are disorienting and can feel unsettling.

Grieving consciously means educating yourself about this unfamiliar process so that you can better navigate it. Understanding more about the emotional tenets of grief can help you accept and embrace these emotions when they arise.

DISBELIEF, NUMBNESS, AND RESISTANCE

Many of us experience some disbelief and resistance to loss. In the beginning throes of grief, this is our brain's way of protecting us from the intensity of emotions that are flooding through our being. You may feel numb and disconnected from reality or like you're watching everything from afar. You may find yourself in a state of shock or utter disbelief that this has happened. You may find yourself shutting down and avoiding facing the reality of the situation. This is all normal. Some losses are too big to feel all at once. And some of us require time to process what has happened to our world.

SADNESS, SORROW, AND ANGUISH

Feelings of sadness are often the most recognized and accepted in the grieving process. Some of us feel them easily and immediately, while others of us take time to find our way to sadness. Some of us hold back for fear that we may drown in the sadness. Some of us have been taught not to let ourselves feel these tender emotions. When we do feel sadness, it is different for everyone—some of us feel a general sense of sorrow, while some may feel lost in a sea of anguish. Sadness shifts and changes over time. Sometimes we learn to incorporate it into our lives and live with it always, and sometimes we move through the sadness and into other emotions.

ANXIETY AND FEAR

It's normal to feel scared after going through a loss. Your world has changed and that is disorienting. You have experienced something incredibly difficult, and you fear going through it again. You may feel afraid that something else will change or leave. You may consider your own fragility in new ways. You may feel nervous about being in environments you never worried about before. You may feel a sense of uneasiness or dread. You may start to look for disaster looming around every corner. You may experience panic attacks. Anxiety is a normal response to change. Sometimes it goes away on its own and sometimes we need to learn how to manage our anxiety.

IRRITABILITY, ANGER, AND RAGE

Feelings of anger, irritability, and even rage are common responses in grief. You may experience anger over irrational things, or you might have very valid reasons to feel angry. You may find yourself angry at yourself, your loved one, medical professionals, God, family members and friends, or even strangers. Anger needs to be felt and explored before it can dissipate. Anger is a powerful emotion that is sometimes easier to feel than sadness or fear. But sometimes anger can serve as a way of covering up more vulnerable emotions that we are struggling to let in. Some people may never feel anger in their grief and that's okay too.

GUILT AND REGRET

Feelings of guilt and regret are steadfast companions to grief. When we lose someone, there are often things left unsaid and mistakes made, and it's common to wonder about the ways that things could have been different. Sometimes holding ourselves accountable for something we wish we could change becomes a way of holding onto the person we wish we could have back. The feeling of guilt creates a sense of connection and can become an initial sense of honoring the person we lost. Finding a new way to hold onto our person can help us let go of the guilt.

FEELINGS YOU MAY NOT EXPECT

Numbness • Anxiety • Forgetfulness • Like you're going crazy • Anger • Insomnia • Exhaustion • Frustration • Confusion • Loneliness • Fear • Isolation • Wanting to be around people all the time • Wanting to be alone • Laughing • Screaming • Not wanting to eat • Wanting to eat all the time • Not wanting to go to work • Escaping into work • Not enjoying things you used to love • Memory loss • Feeling like you can't connect to reality • Stomachaches • Sobbing on the floor • Feeling nothing • Dreams and nightmares • Restlessness • Heart palpitations • Worrying that you're going to die • Worrying that other people are going to die • Fixation on photos and memories of your loved one • Not wanting to look at anything that reminds you of your person • More crying • More numbness • Feeling lost • Feeling scared

Rarely do we submerge in just one feeling in our grief. We swim in and out of so many. Some last longer or occur more frequently. Some are fleeting and ephemeral. Try to embrace all the varied feelings that arise. Ride them like waves in an ocean. Find something or someone to hold onto when they are strong. Rest when they are soft.

Reflection
Draw or paint your feelings. Use colors, shapes, and images instead of words to depict how you feel.

The Physicality of Grief

We tend to focus on the emotions that come with loss, but grief can also be a very physical experience, and you may find yourself surprised by the ways in which your body is reacting to loss.

Think about the act of crying for a moment: Feelings of sadness or even anger and joy can elicit liquid to emerge from our eyes. Our bodies are always responding to our thoughts and emotions—our hearts race, our palms sweat, our chests grow tight, our cadence of breath shifts—and this is no different when we are grieving.

While some of the physical symptoms you experience may seem worrisome, most of them are very normal and will resolve themselves in a matter of time after the initial shock of the loss has worn off and as you begin to adjust to the new world around you. Understanding more about what you are experiencing on a physical level is an important part of understanding how to support yourself through this process.

"Once you start approaching your body with curiosity,
rather than fear, everything shifts."
—BESSEL A. VAN DER KOLK

Many studies have revealed that grief increases stress levels in the body, which can in turn lead to physical discomfort and even illness. Some of the most common symptoms among grieving people are digestive issues, sleep interruption, and "brain fog." Grief causes the brain to send a flood of stress hormones like cortisol and epinephrine to the cardiovascular and immune systems, which can ultimately affect how those systems function.

The stress we experience after the loss of a loved one is broad, and affects our identity, our view of the world, and our sense of safety. This kind of stress can even cause the brain to perceive an existential threat to our very existence. All of these trigger what we know commonly as the fight-or-flight response, causing our hearts to race, blood pressure to rise, and respiration to increase.

Cognitive effects often accompany these physical symptoms—in addition to fatigue and other issues, you may find yourself lacking concentration, feeling confused, or losing your train of thought, all of which is referred to as "brain fog."

Implementing even basic self-care techniques while you are grieving can vastly improve your ability to withstand the intense stress you are experiencing. Adequate rest and nutrition and practices like meditation to calm the nervous system can help us regulate our emotions and support our body as we take time to heal from the emotional pain we are experiencing.

COMMON PHYSICAL SYMPTOMS OF GRIEF

Exhaustion • Brain fog • Confusion • Changes in concentration • Body aches • Heart aches • Digestive issues • Changes in appetite • Sleep issues • Release of stress hormones • Weight changes • Headaches • Migraines • Chest pain • Difficulty feeling pleasure • Difficulty with daily activities • Impaired immunity • Inflammation • Increased heart rate • Nausea • Vomiting • Diarrhea • Heartburn • Irritable Bowel Syndrome • Dizziness • Numbness or tingling • Loss of sensation in muscles

WHEN DOES IT GET BETTER?

It's hard to predict how long grief-related physical issues will last because grief does not follow the same timeline for everyone, but typically the physical symptoms are at their most prevalent at the beginning of a loss and then lessen over time. Occasionally, if grief resurfaces, you may feel a resurgence in physical symptoms. This is normal and simply means you have more grieving to do. And no matter where you are in your grief experience, there are many methods to help support these physical manifestations of grief. For some of us, just taking a few simple steps to care for our physical well-being is enough. Others may need to consult a doctor or seek out modalities like somatic therapy, yoga, and bodywork to increase their health. Refer to the "Tools for Grief" chapter for more ideas.

Reflection

Close your eyes and allow yourself to feel where your grief resides within your body. Are there specific places where you hold grief? How does it feel? Write about these physical feelings.

A Note on Yearning

There is a lake inside you filled with longing. It swells like a tidal wave in some moments, taking your breath away. In other moments, you simply swim within its bottomless depths with no view of land in sight. You want your person back so much that your heart aches inside your chest. You want to rip down the invisible wall that stands between you and them, make your way back to them, any version of them. Any version of you.

You come in and out of this yearning, or you sink into it for long periods of time. You do not feel that anyone has ever longed for someone as much as this. And maybe they never have.

To yearn means to feel an intense longing for someone or something. You are yearning for your person, and the feeling is immense. It's a way of feeling close to your person. It's a way of being in your grief.

There will be times when it feels good to dwell in even the most painful memories of your time together. It helps you feel connected. It allows you to disconnect from this painful reality in which they are not here. Sometimes it will feel suffocating to long like this. You know you can't stay here, but you don't know how to leave.

So just let the yearning ebb and flow. It will shift over time. It's not that you will ever stop longing for your person, but eventually you will be able to carry that lake inside you as if you were always capable of containing so much yearning.

Reflection
Write about your longing. Describe its dimensions, size and shape, colors, and movement.

When Fear Arises

Put simply, loss can be terrifying. And grief can be scary. At times, you may feel frightened in ways you never imagined. The worst has happened. Your person is gone. It can't be so. And if it is so, what else might happen? Your understanding of the world has been irrevocably altered. The fear is real. Your grief is consuming you in ways you did not anticipate. You are not the same. The world is not the same. What can you hold onto?

> *"No one ever told me that grief felt so like fear. I am not afraid,*
> *but the sensation is like being afraid. The same fluttering in*
> *the stomach, the same restlessness, the yawning."*
>
> —C. S. Lewis

You can no longer anticipate how you will feel at any given moment. You no longer recognize yourself. And your grief is sometimes unrecognizable to those around you. You are afraid to be here without your person. You are worried that you will forget them.

This is normal. It's okay to be scared. You are in grief.

Breathe. Move through one moment at a time. Your body and brain and heart are working overtime. Your regular functioning is short-circuiting and reconfiguring itself.

Pull your thoughts away from the future and back from the past. Narrow your lens to this very moment. Breathe. Ground yourself. Hold onto people and places that feel safe.

You will not feel like this forever. You are acclimating to grief. You are acclimating to your new world.

Do all the simple things. Breathe, sleep, hydrate, feed your body, nourish your mind, soothe your heart. Exist one hour at a time. One day at a time.

You are still becoming accustomed to the wide range of emotions you are experiencing. You are still adjusting to this new reality, this new world you inhabit. Give yourself time to acclimate, to gather strength and tools.

Let it be okay that this is hard. Let it be okay that you are scared. You are grieving.

Reflection

Write about or draw your fear. You can illustrate what you are afraid of or describe the feeling of fear itself.

When You Panic

The world begins to swirl around you. Feelings of terror, panic, and desperation arise. Aloneness, meaninglessness, even madness show themselves. You want to run, but you feel paralyzed. You want to go home, but you don't know where that is anymore. You want your person, but they are gone.

Nothing makes sense. This is not a world you are familiar with, and you yourself are not anyone you recognize. It feels like there is nothing to hold onto.

Moments like this are not uncommon in grief, but they are frightening. What's helpful to remember is that these feelings are often temporary. Sometimes they are brought on by a trigger you unexpectedly encounter, and sometimes they are the result of a confluence of events and emotions that simply overwhelm the senses. These moments are part of the process of coming to terms with your loss. Trying to avoid them or prevent them from happening won't serve you. Instead, use ways to steady yourself so that you can ride the waves of these moments, which will eventually reduce their occurrence.

• Use breathing exercises to calm your nervous system.

• Use self-talk and affirmations to remind yourself that you are safe.

• Reach out to a friend or loved one to help you get centered.

• Distract yourself with sensory experiences like taking a shower or drinking water.

• Go for a walk outside.

• Listen to a guided meditation.

Think of these moments of panic as alerts telling you that you might need more overall support from friends and family or talk therapy, or that you may need to be carving out more time for your grief by utilizing journaling or ritual. Think of the panic like a yellow cautionary light at an intersection—your panic is asking you to slow down, be present, and proceed with awareness.

Reflection
Make a list of things you can do when you panic. Keep it handy so that you can turn to it in moments of difficulty.

A Note on Memory

Memory may have never felt as meaningful to you as it is now. Memories of your person have becoming achingly important, and your day-to-day memory may even feel faulty.

You are trying to make sense of something that can't ever make sense. Your brain is working to process and assimilate the reality of your new world, while still dwelling in the past. The future feels unknowable, and there are few familiar markers to guide your way.

You are worried that you will forget your person. You cannot remember where you left the car keys or what you just walked into a room to do. You are afraid that others will forget about your person. You are distracted and forgetful, drawing blanks where there should be information.

Be patient. Make lists. Set reminders. Write down the memories you are afraid of forgetting. Be forgiving of yourself. Ask for help.

This fog you are living in is temporary. It may last longer than you would like, but give your brain and heart time to adjust to all that it is trying to know.

You will not forget your person. Memories may feel blocked in certain moments. Their voice may fade in others. Your heart will rise into your chest, swelling with fear, when this happens. Hold tight, breathe, rest. Your person will return once you move through this acclimation. The memories will still be there, the sound of their voice will echo, and you will never forget them.

Reflection
Find a place—a notebook or a document—where you can begin to write an ongoing list of everything you are afraid of forgetting.

Permission to Laugh

Losing someone we love doesn't mean we lose our sense of humor, and there is so much in life to laugh about.

Laughing in grief is normal and even quite common. You may feel surprised the first time you laugh after a loss, but the truth is that humor and laughter can serve as equal parts coping tool and defense mechanism.

Laughing and using humor don't mean that you aren't also feeling a multitude of other emotions. We can feel achingly sad and still find things to laugh about. While others around you may be surprised to see you joking or cracking up, only you know what your full, dynamic experience of grief is like.

Some of us use laughter as a defense mechanism, resorting to nervous laughter as a deflection tool in times of crisis. If you find yourself resorting to it frequently as a distraction or as a way of trying to make other people around you feel better, then it might be something to pay heed to and work on. But as long as you are also allowing yourself space to feel other emotions and are continuing to face the reality of what has happened, there is no harm in some nervous laughter.

Laughter and humor hold immense healing power. On the physical side, laughter lowers cortisol levels and fuels us with good chemicals like endorphins and dopamine. Laughter also decreases stress and anxiety, and promotes relaxation. Emotionally, laughter and humor provide respite from other intense emotions and can help us put things in perspective and even feel less daunted by the reality at hand. Laughter is also a bonding mechanism for us with friends and family.

And if you're not laughing or inclined toward humor in your grief, that's okay too. However, consider that in the future it may feel good to be able to tap into funny memories and enjoy humorous stories about your person.

Reflection
Consider the role of laughter in your grief process. Have there been times when it has felt good to laugh? Have there been times when laughter has been a way for you to relax and find respite from uncomfortable emotions? Are there ways in which you might bring more laughter into your life?

How Long Does Grief Last?

Forever • Infinite • Depends • As long as one lives • Forever • A lifetime • Proportional • Days • Always • Weeks • Throughout your life span • Three years • The rest of your life • Indefinitely • One year • Grief doesn't ever go away • Six to twelve months • Forever • Depends • Eternity • Always • Five years • Endless • A lifetime • Forever

There is no answer on exactly how long grief lasts. There are theories and studies and scholarly articles offering varying timelines. The people around you have opinions. And you have your own expectations.

It's normal to seek a concrete answer to this question. But before we go any further, take a moment and ask yourself: How long do you *want* your grief to last? Close your eyes and let the answer to this question swim forth.

What comes might be surprising. You may wish for your grief to end as soon as possible. You may hope that it never ends. You may even want both to be true.

The predominant view of grief is that it can last forever, but that it evolves over time. Sometimes this is comforting to hear. And sometimes the idea of your grief lasting forever can feel overwhelming.

For some, grief does indeed last throughout their lifetime, but it changes and grows, and becomes something that we learn to incorporate into our lives.

For others, grief is something that lasts for a period of time and then subsides.

There is no right answer. That's because the dimensions of your grief depend on the relationship you had with the person who is gone. Your manifestations of grief exist within the parameters of your personality. Your space to grieve is only as big as those around you will allow. Your ability to grieve is reliant on your willingness to do so.

And each of these factors play into each loss you experience, which is why you may grieve for different periods of time with each person you lose. However, there are a few intervals of grief that might be helpful to keep in mind.

ACUTE GRIEF is the grief we typically feel in the beginning and encompasses all the shock, anguish, guilt, rumination, physical effects, and reactions to immediate physical changes in our lives. This grief often gives way to a softer, yet heavier version of grief that may stay with you for months or even years.

ACTIVE GRIEF is the grief we typically experience for one to five years after the acute phase of grief subsides. This grief encompasses depression, anxiety, anger, and longing, and it may come in waves of intensity that ebb and flow and change based on triggers, circumstances, and especially around holidays and anniversaries.

AFTERGRIEF is the grief that stays with us throughout our lifetime. Coined by author and grief expert Hope Edelman, the *aftergrief* reflects the way we recalibrate our perception of past events and our relationship with those we lost, as well as how we interpret a sense of meaning around the loss.

In the beginning of a loss, the waves of grief can be quite intense and frequent, but over time the waves grow softer and fewer and farther between. Eventually you may experience long periods of time when you do not feel you are actively grieving. But even years and decades after a loss, you may find your grief rise to the surface around certain events, times of year, life changes, and other losses. This is normal and part of the process.

As we grow and mature, we continually come to understand ourselves and the people we love in new ways, a process that sometimes leads us to realize there is more grieving yet to be done.

Some of us may feel we are "stuck" in our grief, and there are many reasons for this feeling of immobility within the grief process.

Perhaps we feel unable to let go of anger or unwilling to unburden ourselves from something we feel guilty about. Sometimes we are afraid to stop grieving because we do not want to move forward in life without the person we lost.

Grieving often serves as a way to help us feel close to the person we loved, and even close to the person we were before they were gone. This means that the idea of letting go or moving on from our grief can make us feel as though we are letting go of our person and leaving our old life behind.

Getting unstuck in our grief requires considering that there are other ways besides grieving to hold onto our person. And finding these new ways of staying connected comes with a conscious intention to do so—something we must be willing to do.

Give yourself permission to grieve for as long as you need to. Forever. A year. Five years. Twenty. Your lifetime.

Give yourself permission to move on from your grief as well. Moving on from your grief does not mean you are moving on from your person.

Most importantly, give yourself permission to dismiss any notions from others about how long you should grieve. Our culture, our families, friends, workplaces, and communities will all have different ideas about how long your grief should last.

But only you know how long grief lasts.

Reflection
Write about how long you thought grief should last before you knew grief. And then write about how long you want to grieve now that you are doing so.

You Are Your Own Grief Expert

Humans have been grieving for as long as we have been alive. And as such, there are seemingly endless ideas, theories, and advice about how to grieve.

However, not all the advice and theories about grief will be a fit for you. And you do not have to ascribe to any one voice telling you how to move through grief. If something you read or hear doesn't resonate, then discard it and move on until you find something that feels right for you.

Trying to fit your experience into someone else's idea of grief would be like trying to find one pair of shoes that fits every person. It's impossible.

We are all built differently. We come from many kinds of life experiences, different families of origin, varied cultural backgrounds, and diverse educations. We all have unique relationships with the people we lose.

All this to say, be curious about the grief advice you encounter, but remember that you are the expert here.

If someone implies that you should be angry, but that's not your predominant emotion, then do not pressure yourself to embrace anger.

If you see or read something that makes you feel like you should be crying less or more, allow yourself to consider the suggestion, but then stay true to the answer that only you know.

It's normal to want to learn about grief and to try to find a way to help yourself move through it. But it's not very helpful to try to fit yourself into someone else's idea of grief.

Flip through the books you are given. Skim the podcasts you are sent. Glance at the articles. Question the experts. Seek a second opinion. Disagree with someone or something. Return to a place of curiosity about your experience. You are seeking, learning, growing.

You are your own grief expert.

Reflection
Write all the truest things you know about grief.

What the World Expects

The world around you will have a lot of ideas about the way you choose to process your grief. Some of these opinions may come in the form of blatant statements about how you should be feeling and behaving, and some of the messages you receive will arrive in a more subtle form.

Western culture's approach to grief does not reflect the tenets of conscious grieving. Our culture likes grief and loss—and death and dying for that matter—to be neat and tidy and for normal function to resume as quickly as possible. However, this is counterintuitive to the process and only serves to create confusion and dissonance for the person grieving.

What you will notice, or perhaps already have, is that most people you encounter will struggle to adequately acknowledge your loss. Even when they do, most will flounder trying to find the right words to say to you, or they will just say the wrong ones altogether. And while some of the people in your life will be supportive, their ability to hold space for your loss will often fade long before your grief actually does.

It's helpful to understand and prepare for this cultural response from the very outset of your grief experience. And if you have already been living with loss for some time, it can be helpful to reflect on the messages you received about grief and how they have impacted your ability to truly lean into your grief.

The truth is that most of us are afraid of death. We are afraid of it because it is a realm we have no control over. When someone close to us experiences a loss, it almost immediately brings up feelings of fear, which we then seek to avoid, either by distancing ourselves or trying to make the situation okay when it is not okay.

Many people you encounter automatically try to make you feel better upon learning of your loss. Instead of letting it be okay that you are in pain and acknowledging your loss, they will often say insensitive things and ask ill-timed questions. They will offer platitudes and suggest reasons for why your person died or theories about why this happened to you. They will generate ideas for how to fix something that cannot be fixed.

What they are trying to do is make themselves feel better by attempting to make a difficult situation seem manageable. But in doing so, they are probably only serving to make you feel worse.

I'm sorry if you're already grappling with some of these things. You are not alone. If you haven't already, you will eventually meet one person or even many people who will know how to say the right things. They will likely have experienced loss themselves. And these people will be able to commiserate with you about all the wrong things that they too have been the recipient of.

What's important to reiterate here is that only you know what your grief should be like, a theme that I return to over and over again in this book. But sometimes it's hard to remember this truth when you are hearing so many other suggestions from familiar people in familiar places that have otherwise been comforting.

And even though it is possible to recognize when someone is well-intentioned, nonetheless their responses to your grief might evoke feelings of shame, inadequacy, and even loneliness.

If someone tells you that *your person is in a better place*, what you might hear instead is that *they are better off without you*.

When your place of work gives you five days of bereavement leave, you may feel that they are telling you that your grief process should be quick and tied up by the time you return.

If someone expects you to be feeling better after a few months, this may make you feel as though there is something wrong with you because you are still grieving.

When someone forgets altogether that you have gone through a loss, you may think you should have forgotten by now, too.

There are many grieving people who carry some amount of anger, even years later, from some of these hurtful and insensitive suggestions. It's understandable. These things can make you feel alone, misunderstood, judged, unsupported, and unseen.

What helps?

- Set boundaries with people who don't make you feel seen or understood in your grief.

- Decide how you want to respond. In some cases, letting someone know how their statements or actions come across can be helpful. In other cases, it may not be worth your energy to engage further with this person.

- Remind yourself of your truth. Close your eyes and feel your way into the heart of your grief, and give yourself permission to move through it as only you know how best to do.

- Seek and surround yourself with people who make you feel seen, understood, loved, and supported in your grief.

When we allow the expectations of the world around us to drop away, then we are able to gain true clarity and insight into our grief and what we need in order to heal and cope.

Reflection
Make a list of all the actions and words that people have brought you that offered comfort and understanding.

Contemplations

You did not ask to be here. You would give anything to have your person back. You are unsure of how you will survive this experience. You are frozen in disbelief. You are making mistakes. You are angry. You are wounded. It wasn't supposed to be this way. You want to go back to who you were before this happened.

Take a breath. And now another. Let yourself go still for just a moment and listen to the voice inside.

Find a place where you can feel safe and where it is quiet. Let other voices and expectations fade away. Feel supported by the generations of people who have grieved before you. Hold space for yourself. Set boundaries with others. Say no with clarity and kindness. Ask for what you need. Have patience with yourself. Acknowledge fear and shame, but don't let them cloud your vision. Seek courage and hope even when you don't know where they reside.

Just breathe. You do not have to do anything in this moment except breathe.

PART TWO

Engaging with Grief

You are still in the early throes of your grief but not necessarily your loss. Sometimes we take time moving into grief. Your loss could have occurred recently or long ago, but you are no longer in denial or disbelief that it has happened. And while you may not feel ready to engage with your grief, you are beginning to recognize that it might be the only way to survive. Engaging with grief means staying present to all that arises, even loneliness, discomfort, shame, and anger—these are the emotions we feel when we have been wounded, and you have been wounded. But true healing means tending our wounds, no matter how painful the process.

What Does It Mean to Engage with Grief?

Simply put, the only way out is through.

One of the core tenets of conscious grieving is leaning into our grief even when we most wish to avoid it. But there is no going around grief. There is no way to skip past the experience that comes with losing someone we love. There is no quick fix or easy solution.

When we avoid grief we walk in circles, always returning to the same place to find that our grief is still waiting for us. When we can walk forward, even move through the most painful parts of the experience, we allow ourselves the opportunity to make our way to a new place—the other side of grief.

Engaging with grief means staying present to grief even when our instinct is to flee. It means allowing for any feelings of guilt, depression, anger, and shame. It means bravely facing whatever lies underneath those emotions and giving ourselves space to work through what is required to let go of them.

When we engage with grief, it doesn't mean that we are going to feel worse. It doesn't mean that grief is going to swallow us whole, or that we will never stop crying, or that we will fall apart and never be able to function in our lives again.

Quite the opposite, in fact. Engaging with your grief is the way *through* it. Turning away from it or hiding from it requires unhealthy forms of escape and habits that numb but don't actually heal. Avoiding grief causes it to spill out in ways you would prefer it not—irritability, resentment, and anxiety.

Think of that old advice you've probably heard about driving on an icy road. We're supposed to turn *into* the direction of the skid, rather than resisting or turning away from it. Only when we lean into the direction the wheels are already turning are we able to assume control. Grief is like that too. Lean into it.

Engaging with your grief doesn't mean you're going to irrevocably fall apart. It doesn't mean you have to be grieving all the time. It just means that grief is an active process and that it requires dedicating your time and energy to the experience. The energy you devote to grieving may even require that you temporarily alter the depths of your relationships with work, friends, activities, and even parenting and caregiving, so that you can make space for your grief.

Yes, it's true that you may need to seek support to keep your commitments afloat, but wouldn't that be true if you were healing from an injury? Would you keep hobbling around with a broken ankle instead of taking time to rest and heal so that you could eventually resume taking care of all that you take care of?

This focus on your grief is temporary, but if you don't make space for it, then you are likely to find yourself struggling to keep up with all that you are responsible for. The grief we experience in the first year or two of loss, however painful, is a tender window of time. This is grief that is meant to be honored, tended to, and cared for. Doing so will allow you to better resume the life that awaits you yet.

Reflection

Journal about where you can make more time and space to honor your grief. How can you shift your priorities on a temporary basis so that you can engage more deeply with your grief? What kind of support do you need to do this?

A Note About Avoiding Your Grief

It is natural to experience feelings of avoidance, resistance, and even fear within the grief process. Loss brings stress and anguish to our lives, which trigger our innate fight-or-flight response. But fighting with your grief or fleeing from it will just leave you back in the same place where you began, but even more tired and still scared.

For most of us, loss evokes the sense of danger in distressing and unfamiliar ways. When the world feels different, we feel unsafe. When we do not feel safe, we typically prepare to respond to the danger at hand, which is what usually lends itself to avoiding our grief.

Avoidance is further influenced by a culture that wants us to return to normal functioning as quickly as possible. The outside world is urging us to pick up the pieces and move on, even when we aren't ready. And listening to these messages will inevitably encourage you to turn away from your grief, often at the time you should most be engaging with it.

Avoiding grief looks like . . .

- **DENYING FEELINGS**—using efforts to block out, restrain, or deny emotions.

- **WITHDRAWING FROM SITUATIONS AND ENVIRONMENTS**—avoiding places, people, and situations that may trigger memories and/or feelings.

- **PRETENDING TO BE FINE**—attempting to convince yourself or others that you are managing this experience better than you are.

- **PROLONGED DISTRACTION**—engaging in continuous activities that turn your focus away from grieving, and immersing in activities that help you avoid your feelings.

- **PROCRASTINATION**—putting off anything that requires engaging with your grief. This can include funerals and memorials, sorting through a loved one's belongings, and managing end-of-life affairs.

- **SUBSTANCE USE**—using mind-altering substances as a way to disassociate from the painful feelings of grief, which ultimately leads to anxiety and further life disruption. Substances mask your feelings temporarily, but they will still be waiting for you when you sober up.

Instead of avoiding grief, try . . .

- **TAKING BREAKS**—engaging with your grief does not mean immersing in it nonstop. Short distractions like hobbies, watching movies, visiting with friends, and a light amount of work are perfectly fine.

- **SCHEDULING TIME TO GRIEVE**—if you live a busy life or are prone to distraction, you can literally schedule time to grieve. Set aside an intentional block of time to journal, talk with a therapist or friend, look through old photos, or listen to music as a way to elicit and engage your grief.

- **SEEKING SUPPORT**—there's nothing wrong with enlisting a professional or a caring friend or family member to help you feel more comfortable and supported while you engage with your grief.

- **ASKING FOR HELP**—managing tasks such as sorting through your person's belonging or tackling financial matters can be daunting. It's perfectly understandable for you to enlist the help of others with these tasks.

- **SEEKING TREATMENT**—don't be afraid to find treatment options for substance abuse or other addictions that are getting in the way of your grief process.

It's normal to want to avoid the immense roller coaster that grief presents. Anxiety and fear are typical reactions to loss. Fear of crying is normal. Being afraid to fall apart is normal. Worrying that there is too much about your loss to unpack is common. But it's okay to fall apart when you've lost someone you love. No one has ever cried forever. And help and support are always available.

Remember, the only way out is through.

Reflection

Make a list of all the ways in which you might be avoiding your grief. Come up with creative ways to replace these avoidance tactics with healthier coping strategies that allow you to stay present to your grief.

The Effects of Grief on the Brain

The very tenets of conscious grieving are reinforced by the ways our brains function when we are grieving. According to brain scientists, grieving is actually a form of learning—our grief is teaching us how to be in the world without our person.

When we experience a loss, our brains begin working overtime, forming new habits for the new world in which we live, reconfiguring associations we had connected to our person, rearranging our attachments, and determining new ways for us to interact.

Studies show that grief is tied to many different brain functions—from memory recall to our attunement to those around us. And grief is also connected to brain functioning that affects our heart rate, and our sensations of pain and suffering.

When we experience a significant loss, the brain perceives it as a threat to survival, and it employs defense mechanisms that increase blood pressure and heart rate, and even release specific hormones. When we are grieving, many of us undergo changes in memory, sleep, heart function, and immune response. The cognitive effects we often experience, like "brain fog," are simply the brain's way of kicking into survival mode.

Science also demonstrates that the process of grieving is an evolutionary adaptation to promote survival in the face of trauma. When we experience trauma, our brain creates connections between nerves, and it strengthens or weakens already existing connections depending on the intensity of our emotional response. This ability to alter neural pathways is referred to as neuroplasticity, and it allows the brain to compensate for life-altering events like injury, illness, and loss by forming new neural connections based on these experiences—in essence, making it possible for us to adapt to new situations or circumstances.

But the negative effects of trauma and stress are reversible. Strategies that promote a sense of safety, security, and calmness, such as mindfulness, meditation, journaling, creativity, Eye Movement Desensitization and Reprocessing (EMDR), and Cognitive Behavioral Therapy (CBD), serve as outlets for growth and healing, and help reverse the negative effects of stress and trauma.

When our brains are undergoing so much neurological rewiring, our thought patterns can also become disrupted. You may find yourself surprised or even alarmed by some of the strange thoughts you are having. It may help to know just how normal and common some of these strange thoughts really are.

WHAT-IF THINKING

In her famed five stages of grief, Elisabeth Kubler-Ross wrote about the bargaining process a dying person goes through when they are facing the end of their life. They may bargain with the doctors, themselves, and their higher powers. When this stage of bargaining is translated to the grief process, it most often takes the shape of "what-if" thoughts.

You find yourself preoccupied with what-if scenarios. You may find that the last few months, weeks, days, and even minutes of your loved one's life have taken on great meaning. What if they had chosen a different treatment? What if you had called another doctor? What if you had turned left instead of right? What if you had said yes instead of no?

This is a natural response to losing someone you love. Your brain is turning the sequence of events around and around like a Rubik's Cube, attempting to solve for a different outcome. Your brain is attempting to find a scenario that would lead to your person still being here. This is your heart's way of pleading for them not to be gone. This is you wanting them back. This is normal. This is okay. This kind of thinking will ease in time.

MAGICAL THINKING

Magical thinking is the belief that our thoughts or words have the power to cause events and outcomes. This is a common occurrence in children ages two to seven who have not yet grasped how their thoughts and wishes have little effect on what happens in real life. This kind of thinking translates to a grieving person believing that their thoughts and wishes should have prevented an outcome, or that their thoughts and actions could have caused an outcome.

> *"I was thinking as young children think, as if my thoughts or wishes had the power to reverse the narrative."*
> —JOAN DIDION

When you find yourself cycling through this kind of magical thinking, you may realize that you are paying more attention to details that support your beliefs and leaving out evidence that would remind you that you did not have control over the outcome. It can be helpful to ask yourself two questions: *What were my intentions? Did I make the best choice given the knowledge I had at the time?*

YEARNING

This is when we feel an ongoing, and sometimes painful, desire to be reunited with our person. Our focus shifts entirely to what it would be like to be together again. You may find yourself yearning for them at certain times in your life together—perhaps many years ago, or more recently. You may yearn to be with them even during times when things were hard or when they were very sick. Your heart may ache, and you feel preoccupied with only thoughts of what it would be like to be together. These feelings are normal, if not frustrating and sometimes uncomfortable. The yearning is a way of feeling close to them, and it will persist for different periods of time for each of us.

RUMINATION

Sometimes in grief we find ourselves focusing on one aspect of a person's life or death in an obsessive manner. This is commonly referred to as looping or ruminating. Sometimes we are doing this as a way of trying to understand what has happened—trying to know the unknowable. Sometimes this rumination is a result of a traumatic event, or it is linked to feelings of guilt or yearning.

In the short term, rumination is a normal experience, and it eventually gives way to new understandings about our loss. But sometimes we can get stuck in these looping thoughts, which can lead to a prolonged feeling of distress. Modalities like EMDR or CBT, or even just some simple processing done in talk therapy can help us get out of the loop.

Remind yourself that these thoughts are a normal part of grief. Remind yourself that some of these thoughts are not based in fact, and search for evidence that supports a more positive way of thinking. If these thoughts are interrupting your sleep, try getting up and writing them down as a way to release them before returning to bed.

Usually there is a reason for the rumination. Something has been left undone or unsaid, a trauma has occurred, or there is not enough information available with which to come to an understanding about an event. Addressing these blocks is the way to move forward.

INTRUSIVE THOUGHTS

Some of us may experience unwanted thoughts and images that seem to come up out of nowhere at random moments. This can be an unsettling experience but is not uncommon. Intrusive thoughts are spurred on by anxiety and typically are a result of having experienced some amount of trauma surrounding your loss.

You may find yourself experiencing recurrent imagery about your loved one's death or last moments. This is your brain's way of trying to comprehend and process the experience. The brain triggers these intrusive thoughts as a chemical response to the mind's fear response to the event. The imagery you experience may come in the form of repetitive dreams, as well as thoughts or mental content without a visual experience.

Similar to rumination, intrusive thoughts may require additional support in order to overcome them. Techniques like EMDR and CBT are helpful in this case. Although these intrusive thoughts can be frightening to experience, remind yourself that you are safe and seek help to break the occurrences.

DREAMS

Many people experience a vast array of dreams about the person they have lost. Some of these dreams may be distressing, and others comforting. Some people do not dream of their loved ones, even though they wish they could.

Often these dreams can be a helpful part of the grief process, even when the dreams are distressing. Your mind is attempting to integrate your loss, even when you are unconscious. Journaling about your dreams or processing them with a therapist can aid in a deeper understanding of what your dreams are asking you to examine so that you may better heal.

All of these shifts in perspective might sound like a lot. But perhaps there is comfort to be found in knowing that your brain is growing in order to support your grief process. Let this fact serve as a reminder that you innately know how to grieve. Allow yourself to stop resisting and be present to your experience. Even when you think you don't know what to do, there are parts of you that do.

Reflection
Pay attention to the recurring thoughts, dreams, and thinking patterns that are prevalent in your current experience of grief. Are there repetitive thoughts or dreams that are asking you to go deeper in your grief process as a means of growth?

Recognizing Trauma

Trauma is a frequent accompaniment to loss, and more of us experience it than we realize. For too long, trauma was reserved for catastrophic events such as surviving wars, natural disasters, and accidents. But we now understand that trauma also occurs in more subtle ways. And we understand that people react differently to stressful experiences, and some of us are more prone to internalizing traumatic impacts than others.

We can experience trauma as caregivers to loved ones, as witnesses to accidents and illness, and many other different ways in which we can lose someone. Experiencing something traumatic leaves an imprint on our minds, our brains and our bodies, and results in a reorganization of the way we perceive the world. Long after a traumatic experience has ended, it may be reactivated by numerous triggers that cause our bodies and brains to react with intense emotions, physical sensations, and impulsive actions. Left untreated, trauma can last a lifetime.

Signs to look for:

- Difficulty sleeping

- Restless sleeping

- Nightmares and recurrent dreams

- Exhaustion and uncomfortable physical sensations

- Feeling hypersensitive to emotional content

- Feeling disconnected from your body or emotions

- Feeling helpless or frightened

- Experiencing intrusive thoughts or imagery related to the traumatic experience

- Catastrophic thinking

- Avoiding people, places, and events

- Feeling rage, anger, and irritability

- Experiencing terror-filled ruminations

- Isolation

- Fear of being alone

- Avoidance of intimacy

- Aggression

- Self-shaming and insecurity

- Incessant anxiety

If you think you may be experiencing the effects of trauma, it's important to seek professional help. Speak to your doctor, find a therapist experienced with trauma and grief, and ask for support from your friends and family while you heal.

Reflection
What are your associations with trauma? Have there been times when you have overlooked an experience and not recognized all the ways it has affected you?

About Guilt

One of the more complex aspects of grief is that of guilt. This amorphous emotion is one that can root its presence in many ways throughout the grief process. Guilt for decisions we made, mistakes we feel responsible for, choices that could have lent themselves to different outcomes, arguments, hurts, absence, attention given or removed. The list is long and variable for those of us navigating loss.

Some guilt is derived from the desire or perception that things could have been different, and some guilt is born out of very concrete experiences and events. How we choose to address this guilt is important, but so often we stop short when it comes to truly exploring and resolving it. When someone is gone it's all too easy to feel as though we will never be able to resolve the feelings of remorse or absolve ourselves of the things for which we feel guilty.

"Guilt is perhaps grief's most painful companion."

—Elisabeth Kubler-Ross

The part most people miss is that guilt is an integral part of the process of grieving in that it serves as a vehicle for examining our relationships, our roles, our values, and our choices. Exploring guilt can become the very way we shape our new identity within loss. So although guilt is often viewed as one of the more painful aspects of grief, I invite you to look at it through a different lens. Addressing and unpacking your guilt will help you better understand your relationship with the person you lost, and who you will become going forward in their absence.

But just how do we go deeper into something that feels impossible to change? We must understand that there are ways to resolve and make amends for anything you feel guilty about even after your person is gone. We also must entertain the notion that we often hold onto guilt as a way of holding onto our person.

Allow yourself to acknowledge the difference between guilt and regret. Guilt is the emotional response you have after committing a (real or perceived) transgression. Regret is the wish that things could have been different.

Guilt occurs when we hold ourselves accountable for something we believe we did wrong, even when we did not intend harm or even if the situation could not have been prevented.

WHAT DO WE FEEL GUILTY ABOUT IN GRIEF?

Things left unsaid

Caregiving and medical treatment choices

Arguments we had with our person or other people surrounding the death

Not being more available to our person before they died

Not being with them when they died

Feeling relieved that they are no longer here

WHAT DO WE REGRET IN GRIEF?

Not prioritizing time with our person

Not being kinder and loving

Not having had a better relationship

Not understanding just how dire the situation was

Not saying goodbye

Often much of our guilt is for events and experiences that we *perceive* could have been different. We are capable of holding ourselves accountable for a great many things that we often have no control over. And frequently we feel guilty even though we can acknowledge that we acted with good intentions or that we made the best decision we could with the information we had at the time.

None of this seems to matter once our person is gone. The entire landscape of the past shifts to be one in which we now see every moment as leading toward the death of our person. And so, regardless of whether their death was expected, we now view those moments as opportunities we missed to do things differently.

In the beginning of a loss, you may find yourself cycling through these thoughts endlessly, replaying moments and blaming yourself for not making different decisions. But all you are really doing is just wishing that your person was still here. You're wishing that things could have been different, that there had been a different outcome. You are trying to find a way to make an alternate reality come to life. This is completely understandable and very normal. It's you wanting to feel control in an uncontrollable world. It's you wanting your person back.

You may find yourself replaying the entirety of your relationship with your person, examining every choice you made throughout your time together. You also may find yourself hyper-focused on a specific event or experience you had with your person that you wish you could change or do over. You may find yourself examining choices you made or were a part of that affected the outcome of care or attention your person received.

Remember that in the beginning of a loss, we tend to see things through a certain lens. We may leave out memories and reminders about why we made certain choices, had specific boundaries, or took various actions. In hindsight, it can be difficult to accept that we did the best we could given the information we had at the time, simply because we miss our person so much and just want them back with us as they were before.

Within cases of mental health, addiction, suicide, and physical illness, there are often many different and sometimes difficult choices we have to make in regard to our relationships and our ability to provide care. When we lose someone to these circumstances, the process of reviewing history and decisions is enormous and can feel endless. It is almost certain that we may wish or feel that we could have done something differently.

In these cases, it's incredibly important to examine how much you are holding yourself accountable for things you could not have actually changed. Remind yourself of the reasons you made certain decisions in the moments you did, the boundaries you put in place, or the distance you took. These can be difficult layers to unpack, so finding the right help in the form of therapists and support groups can help you process some of the pieces that feel too heavy to work through on your own.

Sometimes feeling guilty feels good because it makes us feel close to our person. But sometimes swimming in all this guilt can make us feel bleak and hopeless. Either way, there comes a time when we know that continuing to dwell in guilt is not a means to an end. Really, it's just a means to getting stuck in our guilt.

Again, the only way out is through.

Assess your reasons for feeling guilty:

- Did you truly do something hurtful and wrong?

- Did you have good intentions or did you intend to harm and hurt?

- Are you holding onto the belief that you did something wrong, even though you didn't?

- Are you choosing to blame yourself as a way to feel control over an uncontrollable situation?

- Did you make the best decision you could given the information you had at the time?

Use the following descriptions to examine your experience and shift your perspective.

HINDSIGHT BIAS is a common psychological experience that causes people to believe the outcomes of past events were predictable, even though they weren't. Take yourself back to the event you are feeling guilty about and try to recall exactly what information you had then. Be careful not to include information you have since gained. This will help you accurately assess your actions. Ask yourself: *Did I make the best decision possible given the information I had and/or the stress I was under?*

COUNTERFACTUAL THINKING is often composed of what-if questions. This way of thinking is the act of assuming that an outcome would have been different if you had made other choices, when in fact, the same outcome could have occurred in multiple scenarios.

STRESS: Don't underestimate the mental and emotional toll that stress can take on us. When we are in a caregiving role or simply enduring a stressful event, we are not always able to think clearly or make logical and rational decisions. Forgive yourself for the stress you endured and the decisions you made as a result. Remind yourself that you were likely doing the best you could.

SHAME is a natural component of feeling guilty about something. Shame is focused on the belief that we are flawed and unworthy and that we have done something wrong. Allowing yourself to release shame will contribute to your processing of any guilt you are feeling. Use compassion and mindfulness to work through your shame. Find someone you can talk to about the shame you are experiencing.

As you begin to unpack the layers of your guilt, you may be forced to confront the truth that there really was nothing you could have done differently, and this can bring about a great shift. Your initial feeling may be an unwillingness to relinquish your guilt because it makes you feel close to your grief and close to your person. But when you release guilt, you are automatically creating space to feel other aspects of grief, and you are also creating opportunities to hold onto your person in new ways.

Reflection

Imagine a conversation with your person in which you can tell them all the ways you wish you could have done things differently. Would they agree? Are they holding you accountable or would they forgive you?

Making Amends
and Seeking Forgiveness

When we can view **guilt as a tool of transformation,** it enables us to explore ways in which we can make amends and seek forgiveness even after someone is gone.

This concept may feel impossible or unattainable at first, or sometimes even long after your person is gone. But if we can acknowledge and accept that our relationships with the people we lose are ongoing even after death, then the ability to grow and change within those relationships remains true.

Doing the conscious work to face and examine the things we feel guilty about allows us to move beyond the static experience that created the guilt and be able to pursue very real opportunities within ourselves to make amends, seek atonement, and find forgiveness.

Making these efforts to address all that is coming up in your grief and seeking opportunities to process it in these productive ways is the epitome of grieving consciously. And this is also part of how we begin to form a new identity within loss, which is why you may feel some resistance to the work.

If you are recognizing ways in which you are avoiding or resisting this work around guilt, that's okay. Be patient with yourself. Come back to the work as many times as you need to. Urgency in processing guilt is only necessary when it is affecting your mental and physical health, your daily functioning, and your existing relationships. And in these cases, enlisting the help of a therapist will be helpful.

Remember that one of the main reasons we are afraid to release guilt is because it makes us feel like we are moving or letting go of our person when we do so. But remind yourself that when we release guilt we automatically free up space that allows us to hold onto our person in more peaceful ways, and that rather than moving on, you are learning how to carry your loss with you as you move forward.

MAKING AMENDS

Even after someone is gone, there are many ways we can apologize, atone for mistakes, and seek forgiveness.

- Write your person a letter or series of letters apologizing and explaining what happened.

- Talk with a person of faith and confess your feelings of wrongdoing.

- Engage in therapy to discuss and process what you feel you have done wrong so that you may better examine the kind of counterfactual thinking discussed in the previous chapter.

- Turn the energy you use to hold guilt into energy applied toward actively honoring your person. Support a charity, volunteer in their name, or do something to make the world a better place.

- Live your life going forward in a way that demonstrates that you have learned from your mistakes.

FIND MEANINGFUL WAYS TO STAY CONNECTED TO YOUR PERSON

Ruminating on the past and holding ourselves accountable for perceived mistakes is one way to feel connected to our grief and our person. However, you can use that same energy to connect with them in more meaningful ways.

- Journal about your person.

- Talk *about* your person to friends and family.

- Talk *to* your person and write letters to them.

- Do things in their honor.

- Look at photos and keepsakes.

- Wear articles of their clothing.

- Embody their values and beliefs.

- Embark on spiritual explorations that create a sense of connection.

SEEKING FORGIVENESS

Forgiveness is something we must seek time and time again in our lives. It includes forgiveness of others and forgiveness of ourselves. None of us are perfect. None of us were given a handbook on how to best live our lives. All of us are thrust into experiences we don't expect or know how to handle. Grief and loss are no exception.

Even though they are gone, you may still ask for forgiveness from your person. Write letters to them. Imagine what they would say to you if you apologized or explained your actions. Interview friends and family who knew them to better understand how they might have felt or reacted.

And find forgiveness for yourself. Forgiveness means letting go of the feelings and emotions associated with what went wrong. It means letting go of resentment and anger. Forgiveness does not mean forgetting. It does not mean denying or excusing a wrongdoing. Forgiveness does not mean letting go of your person. Forgiveness is a choice you make for yourself as you pursue a peaceful and meaningful life.

CULTIVATE SELF-COMPASSION

Self-compassion is a throughline in grief work, particularly when it comes to feeling guilt. Ask yourself what you would think of a friend in a similar position, and then treat yourself as you would treat them. Have compassion for yourself. Extend love to yourself.

Meditation and mindfulness are particularly instrumental tools to use with self-compassion, and there are many excellent workbooks and online programs centered on self-compassion.

This is a simple practice but one that will help more than you can imagine. We can be so hard on ourselves when we are grieving or feeling vulnerable in general.

You didn't ask for this.

You are doing the best you can.

You are not alone in struggling.

Conscious grieving is a practice, and as such, we may find ourselves returning time and again to the work required to move through complex feelings like guilt and forgiveness. Lean into the process. Notice when you resist. Seek support when you feel fragile.

Reflection

Is there anything holding you back from seeking forgiveness and making amends? What would it be like if you woke up tomorrow and you no longer felt guilty?

About Depression

You may already be familiar with depression, or it may be an entirely new experience brought on by your grief. And even if you have grappled with depression before, it may take on different forms within your process of grieving. Or you may not be experiencing depression at all and wondering why.

What is helpful to know about depression and grief is that it is a normal and common reaction to loss. Depression typically sets in as we begin to feel and acknowledge the full extent of our loss. It may come in waves, ebbing and flowing as you move forward into the new reality of life without your person. Often depression sets in at a time when the people around you are expecting that you should be feeling better. But remember that most people are not able to acknowledge how long grief really lasts, and they do not understand the ways in which you may continue to struggle.

It's perfectly normal and okay to feel depressed when you are grieving. Yet there are also ways to manage depression and efforts we can make to pull ourselves out of it.

COMMON SYMPTOMS OF DEPRESSION

- Trouble sleeping

- Poor appetite

- Fatigue

- Lack of energy

- Crying spells

- Loneliness

- Feeling empty

- Lacking motivation

- Inability to feel joy and pleasure

WARNING SIGNS OF DEPRESSION

- Intense sorrow, pain, and rumination over the loss of your person

- Focus on little else but your loved one's death

- Inability to accept the death

- Inability to complete necessary tasks

- Inability to function within existing relationships

- Inability to eat

- Prolonged sleep disturbances

- Excessive use of drugs or alcohol

- Isolation

- Feelings of helplessness and hopelessness

- Suicidal thoughts

WAYS TO MANAGE DEPRESSION

- Ask for help from family and friends.

- See a therapist.

- Join a support group.

- Exercise regularly.

- Eat healthy foods.

- Avoid alcohol and other substances.

- Consult a physician.

It's normal and understandable to experience depression after a loss. However, if you begin to experience intense feelings of hopelessness or suicidal ideation, it's important to seek professional help immediately. There are many people and resources available to help see you through this.

Reflection

What role has depression played in your life before now? Were there aspects of the depression that served you in some way? How did you manage to cope with depression when it was burdensome?

About Grief-Related Anxiety

A persistent thrumming just under the surface, like an electrical current, anxiety often becomes a familiar companion to grief. It's there in the morning when you open your eyes, rides in the passenger seat of your car, infiltrates your conversations and your future planning, shows up to your social engagements uninvited, and keeps you awake in the middle of the night.

Viewed through the lens of conscious grieving, anxiety is a messenger, here to call your attention to matters that need tending. Perhaps it's telling you that you need more support, or it's asking you to address the guilt or anger you are carrying. Sometimes anxiety shows up to help us reevaluate relationships, rearrange priorities, or even release commitments. Maybe it's even asking us to expand our awareness and understanding of death or to explore our spirituality.

While anxiety is often an unpleasant experience, it can be helpful to remember that at its core, humans experience anxiety for a reason. Anxiety is always a part of our lives, serving to remind us to stay on task, to help us prepare for events and experiences, and to keep us alert in times of crisis.

In grief, however, anxiety can grow to enormous and hindering proportions. At its most basic, anxiety is the fear of something real or imagined. So, while it's normal to fear leaving behind a necessary article of clothing when packing for a trip, it's hindering to fear losing another person you love.

Grief can exacerbate anxiety within many realms, some of which you may be experiencing.

- **GENERAL ANXIETY**—experiencing a general and pervasive sense of dread and foreboding

- **HEALTH ANXIETY**—fear about your health or that of people close to you

- **DEATH ANXIETY**—fear about your own death or the death of another loved one

- **SOCIAL ANXIETY**—fear around social situations and interactions

- **PANIC ATTACKS**—overwhelming bouts of anxiety that impair normal functioning

- **CATASTROPHIC THINKING**—constantly fearing accidents and catastrophic events

Grief-related anxiety is a double-edged sword. Left unaddressed, this kind of anxiety can become insidious, taking over many aspects of our lives and affecting our daily functioning. You may be experiencing that now.

Grieving consciously means acknowledging that this anxiety is occurring and leaning into it, rather than away. When we view anxiety as something to fear itself, we only give it more power to control our lives, but when we view anxiety as a teacher, there is much to learn and the anxiety itself becomes easier to manage.

Grief-related anxiety occurs for two main reasons that are intertwined rather than mutually exclusive: unexplored grief and unresolved issues. Grief-related anxiety is like a blinking yellow light at an intersection, asking us to pay attention, look around, and to proceed thoughtfully.

ANXIETY + UNEXPLORED GRIEF

When we have not been able to grieve adequately, anxiety is often the first symptom. Perhaps we have been resisting grief, or the demands of our lives have not allowed enough space and time for us to grieve. Or perhaps we reside within a culture or community that does not acknowledge our loss or allow us to grieve in the ways we need to.

In this case, your anxiety is here to tell you that you need to shift focus and priorities. Maybe you simply need to make more space to grieve. Maybe you need help and resources in order to face your grief. Maybe you need to seek a supportive environment in which you feel safe to grieve. As you create opportunities to better lean into your grief in conscious ways, anxiety will automatically lessen.

ANXIETY + UNRESOLVED ISSUES

Loss presents many complicated aspects that require addressing. You may be grappling with guilt, anger, complex family dynamics, fear of the future, and shifts to your identity. Anxiety is a by-product of avoiding these issues.

Utilize therapy, counseling, and the tools in this book to begin working through anger, guilt, and complex family dynamics. Find ways to embrace your shifting identity, rather than resisting this new version of you that is being called forth. Let grief show you what is important to you in this new world that you inhabit, and don't be afraid to make changes to relationships and priorities. Making conscious choices about how to be present in our lives can serve as a reliable way to lessen anxiety.

TRAUMA-RELATED ANXIETY

Some of us experience the traumatic death of a loved one, and the effects of this loss often require assistance to heal from. Seeking counseling and utilizing therapeutic modalities such as EMDR, somatic work, and CBT are often the most reliable methods for working through trauma.

MANAGING ANXIETY

Working through trauma, unexplored grief, and unresolved issues takes time, but along the way you can be learning to manage your anxiety using tools such as the following:

- **MEDITATION** allows us respite from the painful thoughts of the past and worrying thoughts of the future that provoke anxiety.

- **MINDFULNESS** brings our awareness to the present moment, asking us to rely on our senses, tune into our bodies, and tap into a feeling of connectedness that can soothe anxiety.

- **BREATHWORK** regulates our nervous system, restores our bodies to a calm state, and signals the brain that we are safe, allowing for anxiety to dissipate.

- **EXERCISE AND DIET**: Avoiding caffeine, alcohol, and other substances that provoke anxiety and practicing healthy eating, good sleep habits, and exercise helps our bodies withstand and regulate the enormous amount of emotion we are processing in grief.

Experiencing grief-related anxiety is perfectly understandable. It's normal to worry about more loss. It's common to worry about your health. It's easy to worry that something else catastrophic might happen. Use these worries and fears to tap into a deeper insight into the new ways in which you are understanding the world.

Reflection

Get to know your anxiety. Make a list of the predominant anxious thoughts you find yourself grappling with. Write down the times of day, environments, and situations that make you anxious. Become aware of your automatic response to anxiety. Make a plan for how to manage and support yourself as you move forward.

About Anger

Anger, outrage, fury, and resentment all have their place within grief, and conscious grieving asks that we meet these feelings as they arise, acknowledging the truth of them, and also exploring what lies beneath them.

There is so much to feel angry about when you lose someone you love. You may find yourself filled with rage in ways you've never felt before. You may find yourself incessantly irritable and on edge. You might feel resentment for certain people or about specific situations. When we are grieving, anger spills out all over the place.

Not everyone feels anger within their grief process, so if you are not feeling it, don't force yourself to conjure it up. Your personality, your relationship with your person, and the way you lost them all dictate your experience, and anger may not be part of it.

But for most people, anger is a common facet of grief. And there can be a lot to feel angry about. That your person died. That you are going through this. That people don't understand how you feel. That the world is moving forward without your person in it. That this was not the way things were supposed to go. That other people have it better or easier than you do. That you are alone in your grief. That others weren't supportive or made mistakes. That your beliefs are being questioned. That you don't know where to turn or how to escape your grief.

Anger is often considered a negative emotion, and while it's important to destigmatize the concept, it's also important to question it. Some kinds of anger are even beneficial, and some kinds of anger can be harmful. It's also essential to recognize the difference between anger and disappointment. We feel anger when something unjust or unfair has happened; we feel disappointment when our expectations are not met. Losing someone we love is unfair *and* losing someone we love almost never meets our expectations for the life we thought we would have with them.

Frustration, impatience, irritability, rage, resentment, and pessimism are all forms that anger can take. For some of us, these feelings are completely new and unexpected, and for others they are comfortable and/or familiar. In our anger, we may find ourselves taking it out on family and friends or simmering in feelings of resentment. We may also feel angry at the person who died, at friends, family, medical personnel, our higher power, or even ourselves. While these are normal feelings, they may not be the most comfortable or helpful places to reside.

What we also know about anger is that it is a powerful emotion. In attempts to avoid and resist grief, many of us may find it easier to feel angry than to feel sad or afraid. Anger can give us energy and fuel and motivation. It can get us off the couch, get our blood pumping, make us feel stronger. But when we are being truly conscious to the grief process, we must also peel up the lid of anger to see what's lurking underneath.

Anger is beneficial when it helps us address and recognize negative circumstances in our lives. It can be helpful in terms of addressing and resolving differences. And it's useful when we need to protect ourselves or others and avoid threatening individuals or situations.

Anger is harmful when it impacts our physical and emotional well-being, our ability to interact with the people in our lives, or when it impedes our daily functioning. Chronic anger has serious effects on our health, leaving us at higher risk for heart problems, high blood pressure, and muscle tension. And for those who turn anger inward, the effects can result in depression, anxiety, and isolation.

Irritability, jealousy, and resentment may rear their heads as well, and sometimes it even feels good to dwell in those spaces. In grief, we often feel let down by the people around us, and it's frustrating when people don't understand what we're going through or have expectations for us that don't feel aligned with what we need in the face of loss. Anger is understandable when people say something insensitive, fail to show up in ways you'd like them to, or shut down your grief.

It's also very common to feel angry with healthcare providers who were involved in your person's care and/or death. It's a sad truth that our medical system is not better equipped to support death and dying. As a result, you may feel angry due to the lack of information or attention you or your loved one received. You may feel that you or your person were mistreated or not well attended to, and all of this and more can be incredibly difficult to process. Feelings around these experiences may linger for some time.

However, for true growth within our grief process to occur, we must find ways to release and move on from anger. Much like guilt, holding onto anger can feel like a way of holding onto your person, and much like guilt, failing to seek ways to shift your anger can leave you feeling stuck.

When you feel ready to work on your anger, or when you have reached a point where managing your anger has become critical, here are some methods you can use.

- **ACKNOWLEDGE YOUR ANGER.** Accept that you are angry and don't try to suppress it or pretend it doesn't exist. Allow yourself to acknowledge all that you have lost, and seek more ways to create space for and to face the grief itself.

- **IDENTIFY UNDERLYING FEELINGS.** Underneath anger almost always resides pain and fear. So, for every experience you feel angry about, ask yourself what feelings of sadness and/or fear this experience also holds. And with each person you feel angry toward, ask yourself to acknowledge the hurt and fear they have also caused you.

- **MANAGE STUBBORN ANGER WITH HEALTHY OUTLETS.** For anger that takes time to release, use techniques like journaling, talk therapy, soothing music, and exercise to manage the anger as you continue working to release it altogether. While simplistic and repetitive within the grief toolbox, these outlets will prevent you from unleashing that stubborn anger onto undeserving people and situations.

- **EXPLORE DIFFERENT PERSPECTIVES.** Allow yourself to contemplate the experiences that others may have had or perceived as a way of changing your perspective or allowing for different viewpoints.

- **WORK ON CHANGING YOUR THOUGHTS.** Break the cycle of angry thoughts by actively replacing them with positive ones. You don't have to make the experience you're angry about a positive one—but try shifting away from ruminating on the negative experience and turn your direction toward thoughts that don't bring up feelings of anger. For instance, each time you find yourself replaying an interaction with a dismissive medical provider, pivot your thoughts to a more loving memory with your person.

- **TALK TO SOMEONE.** Talking through your feelings with someone you trust, like a friend or therapist, can help you process and release anger.

- **FIND CONSTRUCTIVE WAYS TO CALM DOWN.** Recognize when your anger is taking over and take active measures to pivot toward activities that calm your nervous system. Yoga, meditation, and walks in nature can help restore your energy to a calmer place.

- **WRITE LETTERS.** Use letter writing as an outlet for your anger. Write letters to the people you're angry with, even if you don't send them. Write letters to yourself. Write letters to your person.

- **AVOID ANGER TRIGGERS.** Make a conscious effort to avoid people, environments, and situations that could trigger your anger.

- **LET GO OF CORROSIVE RELATIONSHIPS.** There is nothing quite like grief to help us examine our current relationships. You may find that there are some people you need to take a break from, limit interactions with, or set boundaries with. Holding onto toxic relationships does not serve you.

- **CONSIDER FORGIVENESS.** Forgiveness does not mean letting someone off the hook. Forgiveness is something you do for yourself, as a way to live a more peaceful existence.

Above all, don't beat yourself up for feeling anger. It's perfectly normal and understandable. You have lost someone you love, and life is not what you thought it would be. Circumstances feel out of your control, and that's difficult to cope with. You are doing the best you can. Seek help when you need it. Forgive yourself for having a hard time during this experience.

Reflection

Get to know your anger. Make a list of your predominant angry thoughts. Write down the people, memories, or situations that make you angry. Become aware of any attachment to your anger. Write a letter to your anger, thanking it for ways it has served you, and letting it know that you are ready to release it.

About Shame and Stigma

Doing anything consciously requires that we allow for all parts of us to make themselves known. But sometimes the parts of us that we keep hidden are ones that carry shame. And feeling ashamed or experiencing stigma around loss happens for some of us. I'm sorry if this is true for you. You are not alone, and you are not at fault. What happened to you or to your person may have been very difficult. But how you choose to process the aftermath is up to you.

In a culture that already struggles to accept death and embrace grief, complicated deaths due to suicide, murder, mental illness, addiction, and even pregnancy loss mean that those who are grieving often receive less support than ever. In these cases, it's not uncommon to find that your community may react in ways that surround your loss with stigma or create a sense of shame for you.

We may also find ourselves encountering self-stigma, which is what happens when we internalize and apply those outside negative attitudes and stereotypes. Deaths from suicide, addiction, or violence often elicit feelings of shame, blame, guilt, and regret. These stigmatized losses fall within the realm of disenfranchised grief, which is grief that does not receive validation from society and often comes with a lack of social support.

The conscious work then becomes about separating your beliefs from those around you. Reflect on how you may have already applied the attitudes and beliefs of others to yourself or your loved one. Step outside the echo chamber of society and allow yourself to reflect on how you truly feel and what you know to be true about yourself and your person.

No matter who you are, who your person was, or how they died, your loss is real, and your grief is valid. No matter what, you have permission to grieve. No matter what anyone thinks, you have the right to create your own rituals and find ways to honor your person. And even if it doesn't always feel this way, you are not alone.

Reflection
Write a letter to yourself, giving yourself permission to grieve.

Secondary Losses

The ripple effect of loss is felt in many ways. The death of someone we care about is the primary event, like a pebble in a pond setting in motion subsequent losses that occur as a result, and sometimes creating the sense that we are losing everything.

Secondary losses can come in the form of financial instability, a lost partnership, shaken or abandoned faith, the loss of hope, future plans, traditions—even a loss of our sense of self. Some of these secondary losses are immediate and some occur over time.

Being conscious of these secondary losses allows us the opportunity to identify them and to grieve for them. And while doing so may feel like a cascade of never-ending grief, trying to ignore the fact of secondary losses only leads to places where we feel emotionally stuck.

It's true that others around you are likely not aware of the broad ramifications of how this loss has impacted your life. They may fail to notice all that you lost along with your person, which can serve to heighten your feelings of loneliness and isolation. In these cases, it's essential to find people who can bear witness to our experience. Grief groups, therapists, and friends who know loss can provide solace during times of cascading loss.

SECONDARY LOSSES YOU MAY BE GRAPPLING WITH

Loss of Your Primary Relationship

You are grieving the loss of your most significant person, who played a prominent role in your life. You are feeling grief for their role in your life, the time you spent together, and the things you didn't get to do. You are grieving the knowledge that the memories you shared are now just yours. You are grieving the support and caregiving they provided you, and the intimacy they offered.

Loss of Family Structure

The entire composition of your family has now changed. It's like removing a leg from a table, and all the other legs have to shift into new positions in order to keep the table balanced. Remaining family members have to take on new responsibilities or roles that are unfamiliar, and many of these shifts can be uncomfortable and lead to friction.

Loss of Social Life

Changes to your social life may occur because of your loss. You may feel unable to socialize or find yourself not wanting to be part of certain circles or situations without your person. Your existing relationships may change or feel different now that you are grieving. People you thought would be supportive are not acting in ways you may have hoped for, forcing you to seek support elsewhere.

Loss of Financial Stability

Many of us experience financial loss with the death of a loved one. We may have lost a primary wage earner, childcare, or even our own employment. We may have incurred debt and medical bills, and sometimes we are thrust into managing finances in new and unfamiliar ways that can be overwhelming.

Loss of a Lifestyle

When we lose partners, spouses, children, or siblings, we experience changes to our lifestyle. You may be single now, or childless, or an only child. You may be grieving being part of communities, rituals, and activities you previously engaged in because of your person.

Loss of Identity

We may have lost a role that we can no longer fulfill without our person. This loss of role can be at home, in our family, at work, in our social circles, and within our larger community.

Loss of the Past

When we lose someone we care about, we also lose our shared memories. If we are left alone after a death, we can find ourselves grieving the ability to rely on the shared memories and experiences that your person held.

Loss of the Future

We have lost our future with our person. We are grieving for the way we thought things would be, for plans we had together, and for experiences we looked forward to sharing with our person. We are grieving the idea of moving through future events without this person by our side.

Loss of Confidence

It's normal to feel a lack of self-confidence in the wake of loss. Your world has irrevocably changed, and you no longer feel recognizable to yourself. You may feel insecure about making decisions or feel inadequate around certain tasks. Your confidence will come back in time, but you may experience an initial period of insecurity and self-doubt.

Loss of Security

You may feel unsafe and unstable in the world following your loss. It's normal to feel a sense of uncertainty and anxiety within this kind of vulnerability. Don't be afraid to ask for as much support as you need.

Loss of Laughter and Happiness

Many of us experience a period of time within our grief when it can feel difficult to experience joy and happiness. We may even wonder if it's okay to feel those things ever again. It's important to remember that we can embody multiple emotions at once. We don't have to only be sad or only be happy. We can feel both at once.

Loss of Health

We may experience physical problems relating to the emotional stress of grief. Sleep and eating problems and exhaustion are common experiences when we are grieving.

In order to grieve these secondary losses, we must acknowledge them. Instead of dismissing them or trying to avoid the painful feelings that arise, lean into the wider arc of loss you are enduring, even when it feels like it is going to swallow you whole. In many ways, the world as you know it is being stripped away, but what will emerge in its place is your new identity, and trying to cling to who you used to be will not allow for who you get to become next.

Reflection
Make a list of all your secondary losses. Create a ritual to honor the loss of each one.

A Note on Multiple Losses

We will inevitably lose many people throughout our lives, and each time the experience will be different. Sometimes we even lose more than one person at the same time, and the feeling of cumulative loss can be intense and overwhelming. You may find yourself suffering a second loss before you have even had the time to grieve your initial loss. When this happens, it is referred to as cumulative grief or grief overload.

When we are overloaded with losses, we may grapple with added layers of avoidance, anxiety, and depression. These are understandable reactions—it is not easy to cope with so much grief and so many different emotions around the loss of different relationships.

You may find yourself preoccupied by one loss and worrying or feeling guilty about not giving more attention to other losses. You may also find that grief over older losses unexpectedly resurfaces when new losses occur. Experiencing multiple losses can also have the effect of changing your worldview, increasing anxiety, and leading to doubt within your belief system.

All of this can have the effect of extending the grieving process, and you might feel like you are stuck in a never-ending sea of grief, but as with any kind of grief, giving yourself permission and space to process your cumulative loss is essential to moving through it.

Allow for different processes for each loss you endure. Let it be okay that some losses are easier to move through than others. And let it be true that some losses may be more consuming and heavier. The relationship you had with the person you lost, the role they played in your life, your current circumstances and personality, and the support you receive around each individual loss are all going to determine the weight each loss will carry.

When you are holding multiple losses, you can grieve for them individually and also collectively. To grieve for individual losses within many, try carving out space to grieve each person in a different way. When we are feeling preoccupied with one loss more than another, we don't have to stop grieving the primary loss, but we can add in time and dedicated attention to thinking about our other losses. Maybe this looks like doing something in honor of each person, or spending time writing and reflecting on each different relationship.

But also allow yourself to feel the whole of the grief you carry. All the losses and all the grief you hold. It's immense and you are carrying so much. You are not broken. You are grieving. You are here in the world without people you miss. As you move forward, take them with you in ways that remind you of what you love about the world.

Reflection
Create a ritual for each person you have lost, and use those rituals to unburden the collective grief you carry.

A Note About Shared Grief

Often, we must share our grief with others who have lost the same person, and this experience can bring added layers of complicated emotions.

You may share a loss with family members, friends, co-workers, or even your entire community. Sometimes there is comfort to be found in this shared experience of grief, but sometimes sharing your experience of loss can be challenging. Everyone grieving the same loss will go about it in a different way, and you may find yourself reacting unexpectedly to their various expressions of grief—feeling angry and resentful or, alternatively, inspired and soothed. You also may feel judgment from others about your grief, which can elicit insecurity and doubt within your process.

Hold true to what you know. Lean into your process as only you know how to do, even when it differs from what others are doing. Find ways to feel supported and centered in the way you are choosing to grieve. Remind yourself that there is no right way to grieve and that everyone around you will have their own process and methods of coping. Comparing yourself to them or internalizing feelings of judgment or shame is not going to serve you. Find your own private outlets and supportive people to see you through your experience.

A therapist once told me that grievers need to protect their peace. In order to do this, you may need to limit interactions with certain people and environments, and even social media, so as not to run up against triggers that leave you in pain or questioning your own way of grieving. Get clear on what *you* need, and give yourself permission to create space for that.

No matter what your relationship was with the person you lost, you have the right to grieve for them and the right to express your grief.

GRIEVING WITH YOUR CHILDREN

Grieving with your children is both beautiful and difficult. The care, understanding, and support they require may feel draining and overwhelming when you are grieving yourself. What's important to know is that children learn about grief and death from the adults around them, and far too often in our culture we attempt to shield children and adolescents. But they will inevitably face loss again in their lives, and the way you role-model grief now will be an opportunity for them to learn how to support themselves later.

It's okay to express your emotions in front of children. It's okay to cry. It's okay to talk about the loss and about your grief. Children comprehend and process grief on a different timeline than adults, so their displays of grief may look different than you expect. Becoming familiar with children's grief through one of the many books available will help you understand what to expect and how to meet their needs. But know that your consciousness around grief will provide space for theirs.

But as with most matters surrounding childcare, you must take care of yourself in order to take care of your children. If you are struggling and unable to devote your usual amount of time and energy to childcare, don't hesitate to ask for help. Doing so will also be a form of positive role modeling.

GRIEVING WITH A PARTNER

Grieving with a partner is a unique experience that can provide an incredible opportunity for connection in some instances, and yet a strain on the relationship in others. In some cases, such as the loss of a child, you are both experiencing the loss in lockstep, and in other cases you may be grieving someone that you each had different levels of closeness with.

When you are grieving with a partner, you likely will notice that you have different styles of grieving. Your expressions of emotion might not be the same, and your needs may not line up. You may also find that you engage with your grief at different times and are not necessarily in sync. Communication is vital. Creating space for regular check-ins and allowing space for each other to express your experience is important. Enlisting the support of a counselor or therapist can help facilitate a more conscious shared grief experience.

GRIEVING WITH EXTENDED FAMILY

When we are grieving a loss that is shared with extended family, there are many layers of the experience to sort through. As with other shared losses, you will become aware of varying styles of grief, different expressions of emotion, and a variety of ideas around memorialization. Some of these differences could create conflict and tension, while others might bring a sense of connection and support.

Check in with yourself frequently within the context of your family—make efforts to stay true to your unique process of grief while also balancing the needs and obligations to your family. Finding someone to talk to outside of your familial circle, like a therapist or a close friend, can help create more space for your personal grief and better enable you to engage with and understand any differences.

PUBLIC GRIEF

If you have incurred a loss that is being grieved and felt on a community or national level, it is important to take extra care to protect your peace. This happens when the person we lost was a beloved member of the community or a well-known figure, or sometimes when our person was lost in a local or national crisis.

When we are in a situation where we must share our loss broadly with an entire community, we may feel burdened with added expectations of how we are supposed to grieve. Or we may even find that our presence is something people turn to for comfort in their own grief. In these cases, you may begin to feel a sense of incongruence within your grief process—torn between the outward version of yourself who is grieving and the version that grieves in private.

Some people use this experience as an opportunity to educate others about what grief can and should feel like, which can feel meaningful. And others of us need to create boundaries and ask for help protecting our peace. Whichever direction you choose, embrace yourself and your grief above others.

SOCIAL MEDIA AND GRIEF

Social media can be a supportive place for your grief, but sometimes it can also be a place that causes anxiety and uncertainty. There are many wonderful grief communities and thought leaders who provide tools, resources, communities, and other services that may feel very supportive after your loss. But some people may feel overwhelmed, insecure, and triggered seeing so many other expressions of grief.

Others find it incredibly helpful to be able to share their grief process openly and talk about the person they lost in these public spaces, but if that is not something that feels comfortable, don't put pressure on yourself to talk openly about your experience.

Reflection

Make a list of ways to protect your peace with shared grief—for example, setting boundaries with people who drain your energy or dominate your grief, or committing to creating space for private grief rituals.

Grief Triggers

A grief trigger is something that prompts an unexpected memory related to your loss. Some of these triggers will be obvious and easy to prepare for, but others may come out of nowhere, causing your knees to buckle in a grocery store or at a birthday party.

Triggers can come in the form of music, scent, taste, images, or even encountering someone who looks like your person. But they tend to elicit *involuntary memories*—memories that you do not have to work to recall, which can make you powerless and overwhelmed with emotion at a time when you least expect it. Once we become aware of a grief trigger, we may become anxious that there could be more at any turn. We want to feel prepared if we are going to be hit with such intense bursts of grief. Yet there is no way to completely safeguard against grief triggers.

Do your best to see yourself through the aftershock of these triggers. Remind yourself that it's okay to fall apart, even when you don't want to. In time, as you become more familiar with your grief, you will find yourself better able to withstand the impact of these unexpected memories. And eventually the memories that once elicited such immense anguish can begin to provide a sense of comfort and connection instead.

When we are avoiding or resisting grief, we may find ourselves encountering more grief triggers than when we are residing in a place of openness with our loss. When this happens, lean in a little deeper, take a breath, and return to the practice of grieving consciously.

Reflection
Think of the most recent time you were triggered. Was the experience an opportunity to address something you'd been avoiding?"

How to Talk About Your Grief

It's highly probable that, wherever you are in your grief journey, you could make a list of all the helpful and unhelpful things people have said and done for you since your loss occurred. Most people are forced to confront their own fears about death when they are trying to support someone who is grieving.

If they have been there themselves, then most of the time they understand what you are experiencing (to a point), and they are able to offer helpful wisdom and provide solace. But for those people in your life who are not acquainted with the kind of grief you are experiencing, it's not uncommon for them to react in ways that feel hurtful.

Being a companion to someone who is grieving requires compassion, patience, and a willingness to be open. It means being open to your experience and to their own feelings at the same time. A helpful companion is able to assume a role of curiosity rather than judgment.

But too often you will find people who are uncomfortable and do not know what to say. They may find it difficult to talk about your loss. They may attempt to find ways to make you feel better or offer generic platitudes. They may expect you to want to *move on*, or to *get over* your loss. They may ask you to focus on good things in a presentation of toxic positivity. All of these methods, and more, usually have the opposite effect of what they intend—they create feelings of doubt, insecurity, and shame for the person who is grieving.

> *"We need words to process our grief, and if the rest of the world is telling us, literally, 'there are no words,' then we are going to struggle and feel alone and abandoned in our pain."*
> —COLIN CAMPBELL, from *Finding the Words*

It's impossible to avoid negative interactions with others when you are grieving, but it's up to you to set boundaries and to let people know what you need. Take measures to check in with yourself about how much you are internalizing. Give yourself permission to feel hurt and angry with others, but then find healthy outlets to process those feelings. Vent to people who get it, journal, or talk to your therapist or grief group about these experiences.

Above all, check in with yourself. Ask yourself:

- Do I feel comfortable being vulnerable with this person?
- Do I want to talk about my loss?
- Do I feel this is the right moment and/or place for me to have this discussion?

It's always your choice how, when, and with whom you talk about your loss. Justifications and apologies are not necessary. How you tell the story of your loss is entirely up to you. How much detail and what is off-limits is also entirely up to you. Don't hesitate to opt out of conversations that feel disrespectful or overwhelming. Ask yourself:

- What won't I tolerate?
- What triggers am I willing to address in the moment?
- Which triggers are too charged to engage with?

Try using these prompts when you feel unable to talk about your grief:

- I'm sorry but this conversation is hard for me. Do you mind if we move on to something else?
- This conversation is triggering a lot of my grief and I need to take a break.

- Thank you for asking about my loss, but I am not ready to talk about it.

- I appreciate you acknowledging my loss, but I am not ready to talk about it.

- *Write your own sentence . . .*

As the grieving person, you know best what you need. If you're able, communicate your needs to those around you. Use these suggestions or make your own list:

- Drop off meals

- Have groceries delivered

- Take out the trash

- Housecleaning

- Take care of pets

- Pick up prescriptions

- Help with transportation

- Help with research and planning

- Help with the funeral/memorial

- Check on me daily

- Listen without giving advice

- Support me through a difficult anniversary

You can also write a letter or make a list of ways you'd like friends and family to talk with you about your loss. Share it with them, letting them know things like:

- I'd love for you to tell me when you are thinking of my person.

- It feels good to hear other people tell stories about my person.

- Please don't ask me about their illness or death.

- Please don't ask me how I'm doing—just assume I'm still grieving.

- I love hearing my person's name.

- It helps when you send me a note simply letting me know that you are thinking of me.

- It would help if you checked on me around holidays and anniversaries.

Changing the culture around grief means that it is up to those of us who understand what it means to live with loss to educate others on how to talk about it and how to support someone who is grieving. But that's also a heavy burden to carry when you are in such a vulnerable place, and it shouldn't be one that you feel required to do. Maybe educating others feels right in certain moments or with certain people, and in other moments you simply choose to take care of yourself by conserving your energy and moving on.

As you continue to grieve in conscious ways, the ability to own your feelings comes naturally, and you will find yourself developing your own ways of asking for help and navigating conversations. Note this as positive growth. You are learning to live with loss.

Reflection
Make a list of all the most helpful things people have said to you, and reflect on why and how you can ask for more of this from them.

The One-Year Arc of Grief

The first year of grief is a distinctive experience, one unlike any other year after your loss. It's a tender and fragile period of time. While there may be painful moments at every turn throughout these first four seasons without your person, it is also a very unique window of time filled with memories, deep reflection, and opportunities to explore yourself in ways you've never imagined.

ZERO TO THREE MONTHS: These first few months are often a cascade of shock, denial, anxiety, and confusion. In the beginning, it can be difficult—even impossible—to fully comprehend the loss itself and understand the full scope of its impact. This period can also be filled with seemingly never-ending practical obligations such as funeral planning and estate management, family negotiations, financial distress, and other responsibilities. Do not put pressure on yourself to feel any certain way. Take things day by day, find ways to ground yourself as you adjust to this experience, and begin the practice of being present to your grief.

THREE TO SIX MONTHS: This period is often the one in which the true feelings of grief set in. Sadness, despair, anger, and anxiety surface in significant ways. This time in the process is often contradictory to the cultural expectations you may be sensing. Community support may have dropped off, and you may feel as though you are supposed to be feeling better when you are actually feeling worse than ever. You are worried about forgetting your person and worried that others are as well. This is a good time to enlist the support of a therapist or support group. This is also a time when the urge to resist your grief may be present, and leaning into your grief, rather than away from it, will require conscious effort.

SIX TO NINE MONTHS: This can be a very heavy time. The reality of the loss—though not necessarily acceptance of it—has set in as you continue to struggle adjusting to the world without your person. By this time, you've also experienced a multitude of firsts. The first holidays and anniversaries without your person, the first time something good happens without them, and the first time something bad happens. This length of time can also mark the longest you've gone without seeing or talking to your person. People around you aren't asking about your loss as often, or they are expecting you to be feeling better when you may be feeling your grief more than ever. Staying present to all that arises during this time may require considerable effort and various forms of support.

NINE TO TWELVE MONTHS: In the months leading up to the one-year anniversary of your loss, you will likely be filled with a sense of anticipation, anxiety, and dread. You may also have the experience of reliving the weeks or months leading up to your person's death. You've also encountered most of the "firsts" and are feeling more aware than ever of life without your person. Lean into your grief to create an intentional plan for the one-year anniversary—whether you choose to honor your person in some small or large way, or seek a quiet day to yourself—getting clear about what you need will help you feel centered.

THE YEAR OF FIRSTS

This experience of "firsts" is an inevitable part of the initial year of grieving, but they can be triggering and overwhelming. Some of these are as simple as a first trip to the grocery store after your person's death, and some are bigger, like celebrating their birthday or yours. Some of the firsts will come as surprises, and others will be dates and occasions that you put thought and intention into.

Give thought to any of these first occasions and consider how you will feel, how you can plan to cope with the day, how you might honor your person, and how you can ask friends and family to support you.

- The first time you must unexpectedly tell someone your loved one is gone—such as a doctor or a store clerk you've had a friendly relationship with.

- The first time you go to an event such as a party or a concert without your loved one—this can cause a lot of anxiety, and preparing how you will cope ahead of time is helpful.

- The first time you travel without them can be emotionally painful and even difficult on a practical level.

- The first time you visit a shared favorite place without them.

- The first time you go back to work.

- The first time you surpass the longest you've gone without seeing/talking to your loved one.

- The first time you want to tell your person about something good that has happened—receiving good news can become bittersweet when you want to share it with someone who is no longer here.

- The first time you want to tell them about something hard that has happened—experiencing new hardship after the loss of a loved can bring up more feelings of grief when they are not here to support you through it.

- The beginning of a new season without them—obvious passages of time, such as the changing of seasons, can serve as a reminder that life is moving forward despite the absence of a loved one.

- Their birthday, your birthday, other loved ones' birthdays—experiencing any one of these birthdays without your loved one present can be incredibly painful. Deciding ahead of time how you want to commemorate the occasion and communicating with other friends and family about your needs is important.

- The first holidays without them—many of us celebrate holidays with our loved ones, and their absence can feel amplified during these occasions. It can also feel difficult to be grieving during a typically cheerful and joyous season. Deciding how you want to spend these holidays can decrease the anxiety that comes with anticipation.

Yes, this first year of grief is born from an experience you did not ask for. And yes, this first year will ask so very much from you. But if you can lean into everything that arises, rather than resisting it, the falling apart will feel more like a breaking open.

Reflection

If you are moving toward the one-year mark, reflect on how you imagine that date will feel. Are there ways you can begin to prepare to meet that milestone? And if you have passed the one-year mark, take time to reflect on all the ways you have grown over time and feel gratitude for all the ways you have taken care of yourself.

About Holidays and Anniversaries

Holidays and anniversaries, while deeply painful, offer opportunities for reflection on your connection to your person, how they impacted your life, and who you are becoming in their absence.

Some of these days and dates will bring all the sharpest points of your grief to the surface. These days are unavoidable. And these days are painful. Some will be harder than others and some will slip by softly, and some will bring unexpected feelings and realizations. Often the lead-up to these dates is more potent than the actual day itself. And sometimes the date will sneak up on you, and you feel it in your bones before you recognize why.

- Birthdays—their birthday, your birthday, other birthdays you celebrated together

- Anniversary of when you met your loved one

- Wedding and other relationship anniversaries

- Anniversary of when your loved one became ill

- Anniversary of your loved one's death—this is also the anniversary of your grief process

- Traditional holidays like Christmas and Mother's Day

While there are no rules for navigating these dates, try to think of them as opportunities to be present to your grief. Use them as a means to honor your person. Lean into them as a time to reflect on who you are becoming. Communicate to those who support you about what you need.

Some days and dates might be quieter and more personal—perhaps an anniversary that only you are aware of and observe in relation to your person. And others dates may be ones that we must share with others. When you have commitments with friends, family, or communities on these dates, protect your grief by communicating your needs, setting clear boundaries, and carving out time for yourself.

If you feel anxiety about these upcoming dates, pay attention to that. Look at the anxiety as a message from your grief, and try to discern what it's asking of you. Maybe it means you need to slow down and take time to be still. Perhaps the date is bringing an unresolved issue to the surface. What are ways you can tend to that issue?

In a culture that usually allots only the initial days after a person's death for ritual and honor, use these anniversaries and holidays as opportunities for more honoring, more ritual.

WAYS TO HONOR YOUR PERSON DURING HOLIDAYS + ANNIVERSARIES

- Light a candle in honor of your person.

- Put out photos of your person.

- Write a letter to your person.

- Cook your person's favorite dish.

- Play your person's favorite music or songs.

- Put out your person's decorations.

- Set a symbolic place at the table for your person.

- Give yourself or others a gift from your person.

- Wear something belonging to your person.

- Ask everyone to bring a memory of your person to share at a gathering.

- Visit a burial or memorial site.

- Plant a tree or memorial garden.

- Light a candle and think of your person.

- Travel to a place that was meaningful to your person.

- Travel to a place your person always wanted to visit.

- Cook your person's favorite meal.

- Enjoy a meal at your person's favorite restaurant.

- Listen to your person's favorite music or songs.

- Watch your person's favorite movie or show.

- Release butterflies or balloons.

- Throw flowers into a body of water such as an ocean, lake, or river.

- Host a family gathering in which everyone brings a memory "to share.

- Donate to a cause that was important to your person.

- Volunteer for something in your person's honor.

Reflection
Is there a way to for you to view holidays and anniversaries as windows that provide a feeling of connection to your person?

Contemplations

Although this is not a journey you sought for yourself, you are making your way.

And while you can't always see very far ahead, with each step you take the path reveals itself a bit more. You are still unsure of where it is you are going and why you are even having to make this journey, but that's okay right now.

Put one foot in front of the other. You don't need to see too far ahead. Take your time. There is no rush because there is not an end point in sight. Don't let your stumbling stop you. We all stumble, and there are so many things to stumble on right now.

Stop and rest as often as you need to. Gather any resources you come across—some of them won't be as helpful as they appear. But try them on, nonetheless. Try on anger. Try on fear. Try on shame. But try on bravery too. And grace and hope.

There is nothing you need to do except keep putting one foot in front of the other. Let your path unfold as only it will. Grief is really just the love you have for your person. And they are walking alongside you even if you can't see them.

PART THREE

Surrendering to Grief

You have moved through the initial experience of your loss. This place you are in has become a more familiar one, even if it's not one you would have chosen. You have received support and reactions from your community, engaged in rituals, and experienced some of the secondary losses and life changes that come with losing your person. You have lived through one or more of the "firsts" and possibly experienced a holiday season or significant date or anniversary without them. You have pushed through resistance and past fear, and you can feel yourself changing and growing. Yet anguish and sorrow continue to persist. It's time to surrender.

What Does It Mean
to Surrender to Grief?

Surrendering does not mean giving up. It does not mean losing or letting go. Surrendering simply means that you stop resisting. When we resist the powerful emotions and life changes that accompany loss, inevitably we create more turmoil, more despair, more anxiety, and more stress.

> "God, grant me the serenity to accept the things I cannot change, courage to change the things I can, and wisdom to know the difference." —REINHOLD NIEBUHR

Surrendering means releasing the perception that we have control over this situation. Control is an illusion that creates discomfort, perpetuates suffering, and creates blocks to growth. And grief *does* offer opportunities for growth, even though loss is almost never a welcome event in our lives.

The answer to your suffering is in surrendering to it. Doing so will not condemn you to a life of misery. Nor will it mean that you are letting go of your person. It means you are leaning into your grief, instead of away from it. It means you are letting yourself change. Let your grief show you what matters. Let it help you process the painful events of the past, and let it help you explore a different future than you were envisioning. Let your grief connect you to your person in ways you've never imagined possible.

Surrendering means accepting the reality that your person is no longer here. It doesn't mean that it's okay that they are gone. But when you surrender, you can allow yourself to be present to your experience, to feel the full range of emotions and reactions that come with losing someone you love. And by doing this, you are giving yourself permission to be who you most need to be in order to survive this experience.

Surrendering looks like being present to each moment that arises, rather than running, distracting, deflecting, or hiding. Surrendering looks like letting go of the illusion that things could have been different or that they will be different going forward. When we step into the present moment, we stop immersing in the past and the future. When we surrender we ask ourselves to just be right here, right now, and to face whatever is occurring right before and within us.

> "Don't look for peace. Don't look for any other state than the one you are in now; otherwise, you will set up inner conflict and unconscious resistance. Forgive yourself for not being at peace. The moment you completely accept your non-peace, your non-peace becomes transmuted into peace. Anything you accept fully will get you there, will take you into peace. This is the miracle of surrender."
> —ECKHART TOLLE

When we surrender to something, we are allowing ourselves to trust in the process. You are surrendering to grief, and you are trusting in its process. Remind yourself that you did not ask for this, and you did not create this. And as such, you also do not have control over the design of how it will play out. You only have to breathe. You only have to wake up every day and put one foot in front of the other. It's an act of faith, yes, but you need not know what it is you even have faith in.

Let go of who you think you should be. None of us ends up as who we think we *should* be. Life rarely ever plays out the way we imagine in our heads. When we surrender to that fact, it allows us to stop all the worry, frustration, anxiety, and self-criticism that we feel when we can't live up to the vision we had for ourselves.

When we surrender and embrace the fact that we are grieving, only then are we able to work through our loss consciously. If we try to control and suppress our grief, then we carry all that resistance around with us into every facet of our lives. We resist joy and pleasure, as well as grace and growth. Unclench your fists. Open your palms. Surrender to what is.

Reflection
What will it take for you to surrender? What forms of support do you need? What must you do to stop resisting?

Who Are You Now?

When we lose someone we love, we often lose a sense of who we are. Our whole life is different with this person gone. Not only do we experience secondary losses of ways of life and roles we have inhabited, but we lose parts of our very identity. Acknowledging this truth and seeking ways to come to terms with your new identity are integral to the process of moving forward after loss.

What is identity? Identity is tied to the stories we tell ourselves about our lives and who we are. It's how we define ourselves in the context of relationships, emotional balance, work, finances, and even location. All of these and more can change when we experience loss. Thus, so does our identity.

The secondary losses that so often occur after a loss can be so significant that our lives may become unrecognizable. In addition to work and financial changes, shifts in family roles and social life, we also experience changes to our self-esteem, our self-clarity, and our ability to manage emotions. These changes can pile up on one another until you are unsure of who you even are anymore. The person you were when your loved one was still alive is someone of the past. This new person you are becoming is unfamiliar and unrecognizable.

This feeling of being unable to recognize yourself can be disorienting and even frightening, but as with any kind of significant change, you must give yourself time to adjust. Try comparing your experience of loss to that of moving to a new town, or even a different country. You wouldn't expect yourself to know the streets or the customs of this new place right away, would you? It would take time to adjust to all the newness. The same is true for your experience of loss.

In order to explore your new identity, begin by acknowledging changes that have or are occurring in your life.

RELATIONSHIPS

This is one of the most obvious places where you are likely to feel big shifts to your identity. If you have lost a partner, child, parent, or sibling, you are experiencing changes that can be hard to comprehend. Questions about who you are now that this person is gone can be overwhelming. Are you still a wife, a mother, a son, a sister? You may also experience changes in other relationships—feeling distance with some friends and family and new closeness with others. You may feel shifts in your social life as well, stemming from the absence of your person, or even your desire to engage with others.

WORK/CAREER/PROFESSIONAL LIFE

There are many ways in which grief and loss affect our work lives. You may need to take time away from your work life, or you may be forced to grieve while working. You may need to work after not having worked for a while. And since so much of our natural identity is tied to the kind of work we do (e.g., I am a professor; I am a stay-at-home parent; I am a corporate leader), you may find yourself questioning who you are within this context as well.

FINANCIAL REALM

Although we may not think of finances as part of who we are, the truth is that our ability to support ourselves and our families has an impact on our sense of self. Losing someone close to us can have vast financial ramifications, both positive and negative. We may be burdened with medical bills, or need to leave a job, or lose a dual income. Or we may come into money following a loss. But either way, changes to our financial security can come with changes to our identity.

SPIRITUALITY

It's rare to go through a significant loss and not experience a crisis of faith. For some of us that looks like turning away from or questioning long-held beliefs. For others this may look like turning toward or exploring new beliefs. What we believe on a spiritual level greatly impacts our sense of self and our view of who we are in the world, and sometimes dramatic shifts may occur within this realm.

PHYSICAL HEALTH

Sometimes when we experience a loss, we undergo changes to our physical bodies in the form of stress, exhaustion, lack of immunity, and the toll of emotional imbalance. You may not feel like you can rely on your physical body to support you as it once did. You may also experience the absence of sexual intimacy or simple caring touch with the person you lost. The way that we feel in our bodies affects who we know ourselves to be within the world.

OUTLOOK AND PERSONALITY

You may experience shifts to your view on life or to your personality altogether. It's not uncommon to experience feelings of pessimism, anxiety, or even hopelessness. If these are not ways you are used to seeing the world, your whole outlook on life might feel unfamiliar. You may also experience changes to how you react to situations, environments, and relationships, feeling a change from who you were within these areas previously.

EMBRACING YOUR NEW IDENTITY

You will never be who you were before this loss. This fact contains its own grief. But part of finding and embracing your new identity will be the very thing that will enable you to regain a sense of self.

And remember that while we can experience so many changes to our identity, for many of us there will remain a core sense of self that we can tap into. Fundamental aspects of our personality will remain intact. Our innate sense of being a son or a daughter, a mother or a father, or a sibling will remain in place, despite our person no longer being here. Our love for our person, and for others in our lives, will not ebb.

Take stock of the parts of yourself that have not changed. Take time to tap into who you know yourself to be, no matter how much is changing around you. Let yourself be curious about the unfamiliar parts of yourself that are emerging. Use self-compassion to find love for this new version of yourself that you are becoming.

And for the changes that are occurring, try to remember that they aren't always negative. While change itself can be uncomfortable, you may find that you are growing into aspects of yourself that you appreciate or even like. There will be new parts of yourself that bring happiness, stability, and even a sense of purpose.

Reflection
Write a letter from your future self to the version of you now.
Give yourself hope from the you that you are becoming.

When Everyone
Drops Away and
You Are Still Grieving

In the early phases of a loss, it may seem like almost everyone in your life shows up in some way or another. Text messages, calls, cards, and gifts and visits are frequent. But what happens when all that attention suddenly drops off?

It's a common experience to feel an abrupt shift in support after three months. Much of this is simply due to societal norms. Unfortunately, in Western culture we do not have a lot of grief rituals that extend beyond funerals and memorials. After these initial rituals have subsided, most people go back to their regular lives, and you may find that they stop checking in on you. This is an experience that almost every grieving person goes through at some point, and it can be startling and confusing when it happens.

Because you have not stopped grieving. In fact, you are likely continuing to adjust to the world around you, experiencing secondary loss and shifts to your identity, and perhaps even feeling some of your deepest grief emotions yet. All at a time when it feels like people are no longer showing up to support you or even acknowledging that you may still be grieving.

Someone you run into at work or at the grocery store may casually ask you how you are, and when you tell them that you're just okay or even not great, a funny look comes across their face. They ask why, what's going on? And you realize they have forgotten that you are grieving. Or worse, that they think you should be over it by now.

There are many reasons this happens. Usually, it's because they are just preoccupied with their own lives. Sometimes it's because they really have forgotten or because they really do expect that you should be feeling better by now. Sometimes it's because they don't recognize your loss as significant or don't think it warrants the amount of grief you are feeling.

All of these reasons can feel hurtful. You have lost your person. Your world has changed. You can't bear the thought of anyone else forgetting your person, or even the idea that life just keeps going without them here.

The cumulative experience of support dropping away can feel incredibly isolating. It can even make you question if you should still be grieving at all. You may worry that your person will be forgotten. You may feel a sense of shame about your ongoing grief. You may feel angry and hurt and lonely. Perhaps you have started to ignore your grief in the same ways others are doing.

What can you do during this time?

GIVE YOURSELF PERMISSION to grieve as long as you need to. Don't internalize the expectations or assumptions of others. Examine any ways in which you yourself have begun to falter in supporting your grief process.

COMMUNICATE HOW YOU FEEL to the people around you. Remind them that you are grieving. Explain how the loss has impacted your life in ways they might not understand. Tell them how they can support you. Ask for help or simply for them to keep checking in on you.

CREATE RITUALS AND TRADITIONS that you can invite your friends and loved ones to partake in. This will serve as a way of creating space for you to honor the person you have lost, and it will also help others remember that you are continuing to live with their absence. Host a monthly dinner in honor of the person you lost and ask people to share memories. Attend a sporting event they enjoyed, post photos of them online, volunteer somewhere in their honor. Involving your friends and family in rituals like this is an indirect way to remind them that you are still grieving and also gives them an opportunity to provide their support.

SEEK SUPPORT from places and people who will acknowledge your loss and understand your grief process. Reach out to friends who have experienced their own grief and loss. Read memoirs or self-help books about loss. Join a grief group. Find a therapist. Doing these things will help you feel less alone in your grief and will also validate your experience.

Reflection
How can you recommit to allowing yourself space to grieve, to leaning into moments of grief, dates that bring reflection, and growth that is occurring?

Coping with Insensitivity

When we choose to consciously support our grief process, it doesn't mean everyone around us will be doing the same. You understand by now that people say hurtful things. But with your emotions running just under the surface, even the smallest comments or actions have left you feeling angry, disappointed, or deeply hurt.

Even when you are someone who is usually good at ignoring the slights of others, grief can make even the most well-intentioned comment feel like a dagger. Often these painful remarks or actions stem from social prejudices, the commenter's own fear of death, simple misconceptions, or just a place of utter naivete.

Most people really do mean well, but when outsiders are confronted with your loss and attempt to offer consoling words, they tend to misstep more often than not. Add to that your heightened sensitivity, and it can become a lethal combination that leaves you roiling in fury and pain.

Often the first instinct people have when they encounter someone who is hurting is to try to "fix" the situation. But grief isn't something that can be fixed.

Someone who truly knows how to be supportive should not try to fix your grief. They shouldn't tell you what to do or try to make things better by invalidating your feelings. A supportive person should be able to recognize your grief and hold space for the multitude of feelings you are experiencing. They should give you as much time as you need to process your loss and be able to meet you where you are along the way.

EXAMPLES OF HELPFUL COMMENTS AND ACTIONS

- "I am sorry for your loss."

- "I wish I knew the right words."

- "I care about you and how you're feeling."

- "I don't know how you feel but I'm here for you."

- "You and your person are in my thoughts."

- "I am here whenever you need me."

- Giving you a hug.

- Just being present with you.

EXAMPLES OF HURTFUL COMMENTS AND ACTIONS

- "Your person is in a better place."

- "It was your person's fault."

- "You should try to forget about your person."

- "You shouldn't be so sad."

- Comments cased within a religion or doctrine you do not adhere to.

- "Everything happens for a reason."

- "You have to be strong."

- "They wouldn't want you to be sad."

- "You should be over it by now."

- Saying nothing and not acknowledging your loss.

- "You should focus on positive things."

- Comparing your loss to something else.

- "You need to move on."

- "It was their time."

- "You're being selfish."

- Avoiding you.

- "At least they're out of pain."

- "I couldn't cope with what you're going through."

- "Time heals all wounds."

- "There's a reason for everything."

- "At least they had a long life."

- "I hope you get over this soon."

WAYS TO COPE WITH INSENSITIVITY

If you receive a hurtful comment or you feel that someone is being disrespectful, there are various ways you can cope.

IGNORE: Take a moment to decide if your anger is worth your energy. Did the commenter have good intentions or were they truly being hurtful? If they didn't mean it, then try to remember that you have enough going on and it may be better to just let it go. Even if they were being intentionally hurtful, it might not be worth your energy to hold onto it. Set some boundaries and take a break from this person.

BE HONEST: It's always an option to tell someone that their comments or attitude are hurtful. This may feel important if it is someone you're close with or if they continue to repeat words that are causing you distress. Being honest can help them to better support you.

BE DIRECT: Tell them that their comments or actions are upsetting you and adding to your emotional burden. Let them know that regardless of what they believe, your grief is valid and real.

SET BOUNDARIES: Avoid negative people or specific individuals who continue to hurt you. Surround yourself with loving and nurturing people who can support your grief process.

FIND A GRIEF COMMUNITY: You may find it helpful to spend time with others who are grieving. You don't necessarily have to talk about your grief, but being around others who understand can feel comforting.

TALK TO A THERAPIST: If you can't stop thinking about something someone has done or said to you, it might be helpful to talk through it with a trained professional in order to move through the pain.

Reflection

Write a letter to someone who said something insensitive to you. (You don't need to send it.) Tell them why their remarks were hurtful and describe what would be helpful to say to someone who is grieving.

Recognizing
Destructive Tendencies

Choosing to be conscious and intentional within our grief process isn't always easy. Often it requires looking at painful truths and allowing ourselves to experience feelings of intense anguish, overwhelm, and fear.

When we are ill-equipped to withstand these emotions, it's not uncommon to find ourselves tempted to soothe or distract ourselves with destructive behavior. This can happen when we have a history of relying on unhealthy coping methods, or even if we don't.

What's important is that you meet yourself with compassion in these moments. Recognize the behavior you are engaging in or tempted by and take time to understand why. This often requires acknowledging the pain and complexity of grief, and it also means seeking support and asking for help.

In the initial period following a loss and in the beginning throes of grief, unhealthy behavior might seem okay as a temporary indulgence, but these behaviors often lead to long-term habits with detrimental consequences:

• Smoking

• Overeating

• Drinking alcohol

• Over-the-counter drug overuse and abuse

• Illegal drug abuse

• Excessive exercise

- Eating disorders—bulimia, anorexia nervosa, binge eating

- Workaholism

- Anger issues

- Excessive fantasy (video games, computers, books, television, movies)

- Isolation and avoidance

- Sex

- Shopping

The problem with these behaviors is that they may appear to work initially by providing relief from your grief or enhancing your mood, but the relief doesn't last, and these distractions don't address the emotional turmoil you are experiencing. Choosing to indulge in these behaviors can cause more problems than they solve, and can eventually lead to delayed and complicated grief.

Try replacing unhealthy behavior with the following:

- Moderate exercise

- Meditation

- Mindfulness

- Rest

- Being of service

- Therapy and counseling

- Affirmations

- Visualizations

- Journaling

Don't be afraid to seek help for overcoming destructive tendencies. If you can allow yourself to be conscious to everything you are experiencing, even these unhealthy coping methods, you will be able to find compassion for yourself. And self-compassion will give you permission to ask for help.

Reflection
Make a list of your destructive tendencies. Write down the thoughts and feelings that drive you to these behaviors and then create a list of healthy outlets for difficult moments.

Navigating
Professional Grief Support

What does it **mean to feel supported in your grief?** It means you are met with understanding, empathy, and permission to show up and to grieve in all the ways you need to. It can be painful to realize that not all the people in your life are able to provide support in these ways, but this is why it can be helpful, or even vital, to reach out for professional forms of support.

Finding what's right for you might take some trial and error, because what works for each person's individual grief process always looks a little different.

WHY SEEK PROFESSIONAL GRIEF SUPPORT?

- If you are feeling uncomfortable sharing your grief around the people closest to you.

- If you do not feel safe or supported enough in your grief.

- If you are struggling with persistent feelings of guilt, remorse, anger, or anxiety.

- If you simply want to connect with others who are going through something similar.

WHEN TO SEEK PROFESSIONAL GRIEF SUPPORT

- You can seek grief support at any time—whether your loss happened days ago or even decades ago.

- Some programs may require that you be a certain amount of time out from your loss or even that your loss be within the last few years—if this is the case, keep searching for one that fits your parameters.

- There are many available coaches, counselors, and therapists who will see you within days of experiencing a loss.

- When seeking support for a loss that is far in the past, interview therapists and counseling professionals to make sure they have experience working with long-term loss.

GRIEF SUPPORT GROUPS

- Grief support groups (either in-person or virtual) offer the opportunity to meet in a small group setting with others who are grieving. These groups are almost always facilitated by a trained professional and are frequently offered by individual therapists, grief centers, faith-based communities, and healthcare organizations.

- Support groups offer the opportunity to learn more about the grief process, talk about your loss, and connect with others who are going through something similar.

- These groups might be open-ended or run for a limited length of time. Some groups may cost money, and some are offered free of charge.

- While in-person groups are wonderful, there is more availability online, and even a virtual support setting can provide much-needed solace.

- Numerous grief support groups are found in most communities and are almost always available online. Trying searching "grief support groups near me," or contact your local hospice, community center, or place of worship.

- The most helpful grief support groups are those in which you can be with other grievers who have experienced a similar loss (e.g., loss to suicide, loss of parent, loss of child) or with others who are a similar age to you even if they do not share your same type of loss. But even a general grief support group that is open to anyone working through any kind of loss can be a beneficial place.

- Please note that while grief support groups can be incredibly healing on many levels, they are not always right for everyone. For some, being around other people talking about loss is too triggering or overwhelming. Or you just may find that the group attendees or even the facilitator does not feel like the right fit for you. Seek out other groups if you are so inclined, but do not pressure yourself to attend one that isn't a match.

GRIEF THERAPY, COUNSELING, AND COACHING

- Grief therapy, grief counseling, and grief coaching are healing ways to work through some of the larger issues of loss. You will be able to process secondary losses, sort through issues around your relationship with your person, talk about how their death is affecting your life, and also work to process feelings of anger, guilt, and anxiety.

- One-on-one therapy is best for people who have a lot to process, for those who do not feel comfortable in a group setting, and for those who may need more time to process their grief than a support group may provide.

- Grief therapists and counselors have similar training and skill sets that enable them to work with complex issues and complicated losses. Grief coaches in particular will focus on helping you explore and establish your identity within loss and create goals for positive growth, whereas a therapist may delve into your past in order to explore your present experience. Don't be afraid to interview different practitioners and ask them about their specialties and ways of working with clients.

- It's perfectly normal to have a regular therapist and also seek out additional short-term grief therapy or coaching at the same time. Grief is a very particular experience that only someone trained in grief and loss will be truly skilled with.

- There should be numerous grief counselors, coaches, and therapists available in your community or online. Trying searching "individual grief support near me."

- As with any professional, finding the right person is imperative. Don't be afraid to set up a consultation to see if they can provide what you are looking for, and it's always good practice to give a new practitioner at least three sessions to decide if it's the right fit.

GRIEF BOOKS AND WORKBOOKS

- Books about grief and loss are bountiful. Try a simple search for "grief books" or narrow your search to fit your type of loss by searching something like "books for widows" or "books about child loss."

- It's unlikely that there will be one exact book that perfectly suits your grief experience. Read or skim through several different books and take bits and pieces that are helpful to you. Discard anything that isn't a fit. Do not pressure yourself to fit into the mold of any one type of advice.

- General self-help books about grief and loss can be useful in normalizing your experience and providing coping techniques.

- Specific books about your type of loss will help provide even more in-depth knowledge, techniques, and advice suited specifically to what you are going through.

- There are many excellent workbooks that provide exercises, journal prompts, and meditations.

- Many grief journals are available that provide prompts for you to explore writing through loss.

- Reading memoirs written by people who have gone through loss can also be incredibly healing and give you the sense that you are not alone, as well as provide testimony about surviving this experience.

ONLINE GRIEF COMMUNITIES

- Online grief communities have become a popular form of grief support and are readily available worldwide at any time.

- Some communities are open to anyone grieving any kind of loss, and some are open to people grieving specific losses (e.g., Motherless Daughters).

- Some online grief communities are moderated by a trained professional, and others consist of only grieving people.

- Some online communities feature open or themed discussions, some are focused on writing about loss, and some simply have message boards where you can share about your loss or respond to things others have shared.

- Try a simple search for "online grief communities."

GRIEF RETREATS

- Grief retreats can be a wonderful opportunity for an intensive healing experience.

- Grief retreats typically take place over several days in a secluded and relaxing location, during which you will participate in various forms of group therapy, workshops, meditation, yoga, journaling, and sharing about your loss with a skilled facilitator.

- Grief retreats allow for the opportunity to process a lot of your loss in a short period of time, as well as to commune with others who are experiencing something similar.

- Grief retreats can be costly and may be in locations far from where you live.

- Some grief retreats are oriented to specific losses or religions, or can even incorporate psychedelics or unconventional healing modalities. Only attend something that feels comfortable for you.

- Try a simple online search for "grief retreats" to research and find the one that is right for you.

A NOTE ABOUT PSYCHIC MEDIUMS

- While psychic mediums are not for everyone, it is important to include here because a great many people seek out sessions with mediums when they are grieving, and there are a few things to consider.

- Psychic mediums may indeed provide a healing experience for some people, but they should not be a replacement for true grief support or for those seeking to process complicated feelings or losses that require a therapist or skilled support group.

- Psychic mediums can provide a sense of connection that can act as a start for you to create your own personal sense of lasting connection with your person.

- Psychic mediums are hit or miss. Try to see someone who comes recommended or referred by a reputable source.

- What a psychic medium tells you should not necessarily be taken as truth or fact. If they tell you something helpful, that can be healing. However, if a psychic tells you something that does not fit with your understanding of your person or your loss, please discard it and process the experience with someone skilled in grief work.

FAITH-BASED SUPPORT

There are vast opportunities for grief support within religious organizations and places of worship. You may have already relied upon or interacted with clergy members as you chose ways to honor and memorialize your loved one. Reaching out for more ongoing support is almost always an option—even if it's been some time since you felt connected to your faith. Though clergy members won't necessarily have the professional qualifications to diagnose complicated mental disorders, they are typically well-versed in grief and can offer one-on-one support, community support, and provide additional resources.

Reflection
Make a list of the ways in which you need to feel supported in your grief, and assess the offerings above to see which one seems like the best match.

Further Notes on Anxiety

While anxiety can be a common occurrence immediately following a loss, some of us do not encounter it until deeper into our experience of grief, once the initial feelings of shock and denial have worn off. Anxiety is tricky because it can be insidious, meaning that once it surfaces, it may grow or intensify depending on how you choose to manage it.

Sometimes we begin to experience anxiety later in a grief process because we have been suppressing our grief, and the unexplored emotions around your loss are spilling out in a manifestation of fear and unease.

For others, we find ourselves becoming more anxious as the reality of our loss sets in and we are confronted with the realization that our time here is finite, and we are not in control of how long we have.

Others experience recurrent anxiety due to unprocessed trauma around the loss or neglected feelings of guilt and remorse about our relationship with the person we lost or the way their death unfolded.

And still others experience anxiety as a result of intense secondary losses that occur within our lives affecting our health, financial stability, and social support.

What is important to know about grief-related anxiety is that it is not typically something that goes away on its own. We must learn to manage anxiety in order to diminish it. Coping tools and skills must be implemented. Grief and trauma must have outlets and be adequately processed.

If you find yourself experiencing an uptick in your anxiety levels, or your anxiety is continuing to simmer and impede your functioning, then it is time to find ways to manage it and ultimately diminish it.

The goal with anxiety is not to get rid of it altogether. Normal anxiety is a useful tool in our day-to-day lives and helps us function. But anxiety that keeps you up at night, prevents you from accomplishing daily tasks, affects your relationships, or consumes you on a regular basis is debilitating and can worsen if not managed or treated.

Social anxiety, health anxiety, death anxiety (yours or others), catastrophic thoughts, and panic attacks are common experiences of this kind of intensified anxiety. There are different methods to work with each one, but each type of anxiety requires facing it and acknowledging it.

EFFECTIVE METHODS FOR MANAGING ANXIETY

- Eye Movement Desensitization and Reprocessing (EMDR)

- Cognitive Behavioral Therapy (CBT)

- Talk therapy

- Grief support groups

- Meditation and mindfulness

- Anxiety workbooks

- Prescribed medication

Do not feel ashamed if you are experiencing anxiety. Seek all the help and advice and treatment you need. It is normal and okay to feel anxiety after the immense experience of loss and all that accompanies it. But know that anxiety can be managed and treated, and you can live a more peaceful existence.

Practicing Self-Compassion

Grieving consciously requires using compassion for ourselves as we encounter all that loss asks us to explore. To release guilt, dismantle anger, and navigate our interpersonal relationships within grief, we quite often run up against unsettling aspects of ourselves. If we cannot meet those parts of ourselves with compassion, we will falter in the work and make very little progress.

This is why self-compassion is one of the cornerstones of conscious grieving. You must meet your experience with as much self-love and compassion as possible in order to allow for the possibility of growth.

We cannot will ourselves to the other side of grief without meeting ourselves first where we are. So wherever you are, whatever you are grappling with, however much you are struggling, let that be okay.

You did not ask for this. You did not create this.
You are doing the best you can.

Make that a mantra if you must.

I did not ask for this. I did not create this. I am doing the best I can.

Repeat those three sentences morning, noon, and night. Because the truth is that you are probably repeating a lot more negative thoughts on a regular basis. You may be telling yourself that you should have it together by now or that you should be doing better. Maybe you think you should be crying less or more. Perhaps you're internalizing outside judgment about your grief process. Maybe you are pretending to be more healed than you really are.

You did not ask for this. You did not create this.
You are doing the best you can.

Self-compassion is essential to your sense of stability, peace, and growth through this process. However, self-compassion does not always come naturally. Instead, we tend to be self-critical and hard on ourselves, especially when we are vulnerable or struggling. These are the times we need kindness and understanding most of all. Self-compassion must become a practice.

"Talk to yourself like you would talk to someone you love."
—BRENÉ BROWN

TENETS OF SELF-COMPASSION

MINDFULNESS: Invite yourself to be present to your thoughts, feelings, and circumstances, whatever they may be.

CONNECTEDNESS: Allow yourself to feel connected to a larger sense of humanity, and remind yourself that everyone experiences suffering at some time or another. You are not alone.

SELF-KINDNESS: Express love and compassion toward yourself. Lean away from negative self-talk and toward positive affirmations.

HOW WOULD YOU TREAT A FRIEND?

If you find it challenging to extend this kind of compassion toward yourself, try thinking about times when a close friend has struggled with something or felt badly about themselves. How did you respond to them? Think about what you said and did, and the compassion you felt for them.

Now think about what you are currently struggling with or feeling badly about. Notice any negative thoughts and feelings you currently have toward yourself.

Next, think about the difference between how you reacted to your friends who have struggled as opposed to how you are reacting to yourself.

Finally, talk to yourself in the supportive and reassuring ways that you have done with your friends.

MINDFULNESS FOR SELF-COMPASSION

Use the following steps to cultivate a mindful moment of self-compassion:

1. Acknowledge that the present moment is painful. Recognize that you are suffering. Instead of dismissing these feelings, accept them as part of your truth.

2. Remind yourself that suffering and pain are unavoidable parts of life. Everyone experiences difficult moments and periods of anguish. Remind yourself that you are not alone in what you are going through.

3. Repeat a mantra to yourself, such as:

It's okay that I'm having a hard time.

Let me be kind to myself.

Let me receive the support I need.

Let me accept myself as I am.

Let me have compassion for myself.

LETTER WRITING FOR SELF-COMPASSION

Writing letters to ourselves is a form of self-compassion. It will help you express emotions and talk to yourself in an understanding and forgiving way. Try writing one of these letters once a week or more if needed.

1. Bring to mind whatever it is you are being hard on yourself about. Examples could be thinking you should be stronger, grieving less or more, or not as angry or sad.

2. Now write a letter to yourself from the perspective of a friend or someone who deeply cares for and loves you. Write everything they would say to you, all the ways they might comfort you, and all the ways they would be understanding of what you're going through.

Remember that having compassion for yourself does not mean you have to be perfect, or that you have to be different or better. It does not mean you are not accountable for your misdeeds or wrong-doings. Being self-compassionate simply means that you are accepting yourself as who you are in this moment, and extending love and understanding toward yourself as you make your way through this grief.

Reflection

Write a self-compassion letter to yourself, extending all the same kindness and love that you would to a friend who was going through what you are experiencing.

Thoughts → Emotions → Behavior

The constructs of our emerging grief identity are built on a chain of thoughts, emotions, and behavior. And if we are not present to our experience, this chain can lead us into versions of ourselves that do not serve us.

THOUGHTS

When we wake up in the morning our brains come alive with a jumble of thoughts that continue throughout the day. It's understandable that the landscape of our thoughts takes on new forms when we are grieving. Everything from the practicalities of our daily obligations to the bigger picture of our life now that our person is gone—there are so many things running through our heads. Some thoughts are loud; others are quieter. Some thoughts play on repeat, and some are composed of jumbled fragments that are barely coherent. Your loss might be the first thing you think about in the morning, and the last before bed.

EMOTIONS

Each thought we have has the potential to elicit an emotion. A pleasant thought about your person may bring you feelings of comfort while a painful memory might provoke anxiety. Thoughts about your daily obligations may make you feel overwhelmed, and thoughts about a person you will see may evoke resentment. Some thoughts will flick by and register very little emotional response, and other thoughts will leave you feeling overcome with sadness or guilt.

BEHAVIOR

The emotions we feel frequently direct our actions and behavior. Feelings of sadness may influence your decision to stay in bed all day, while feelings of anger may provoke you to drive recklessly or snap at someone. Feelings of anxiety can lead to substance abuse, and guilt can drive us to treat ourselves in neglectful ways. We all exist on a spectrum when it comes to our ability to regulate our responses to emotion, some of us better at it than others.

THOUGHTS → EMOTIONS → BEHAVIOR

You can see how after loss, when our thoughts are dominated by grief, we can become overwhelmed by powerful emotions that dictate how we move through our days.

When we are grieving, we naturally spend a lot of time thinking about the past and a lot of time thinking about the future, neither of which are the present moment. Thus we are constantly reacting to perceptions of reality and thoughts that are not necessarily rooted in probability.

Learning how to recognize these triggering thoughts, manage the ensuing emotions, and choose healthy behavior and reliable actions is an essential part of riding the waves of grief and staying grounded within grief.

All easier said than done, but think of this growing awareness as a practice.

Even when we understand that thoughts based in the past may stir up feelings of anguish, anger, fear, guilt, and anxiety, we may find ourselves dwelling in those spaces nonetheless, seeking comfort and connection to what once was. Or you may find yourself confronted with an event that leads you down a path of worrying about the future without your person.

When you catch yourself in these places, remember that thoughts about the past and the future are not based in reality. You can *imagine* what it will feel like to attend a wedding or experience a holiday without your person, but you do not really *know* what it will be like or how it will feel. The experience could be better or worse than what you imagine.

It would be impossible to avoid thoughts of the past and future, nor should we avoid them altogether, but we can begin to recognize when these thoughts are stirring up emotions that we are not prepared to manage, with ensuing actions that might have negative consequences.

It's also common to fall into patterns of worst-case-scenario thinking and attempt to use catastrophic thinking as a way to feel in control. We assume that if we imagine everything that could go wrong, then we will be prepared for it, but really we are just keeping ourselves in a perpetual state of heightened awareness and increasing our anxiety level.

When we reside in a place of unexamined grief, we are subject to the mercy of this thought→emotion→behavior chain. But when we choose to grieve consciously, we seek knowledge and understanding of our experience so that we may unburden ourselves from unnecessary emotional distress and free ourselves of unhealthy coping methods.

Try replacing negative and painful thoughts with calming mantras. Interrupt patterns of excessive worry with meditation. Find ways to take breaks from dwelling in thoughts of the past or future so that you can allow space for moments of peace and rest. Yoga, meditation, and mindfulness are all techniques that bring our awareness to the present moment. Mantras can remind you that you are safe and taken care of. Self-compassion will see you through moments of struggling with this practice.

Reflection

Make an attempt to notice your predominant thought, emotion, and behavior patterns and use the methods suggested above to practice a new habit of awareness.

Integrating Your Loss

Grieving consciously means allowing yourself to integrate this loss into your life. It never has to be okay that your person died. You don't ever have to get *over* it. And you don't need to reach some mythical place of acceptance in order to heal.

What you are working toward is learning how to live with your loss. Living with loss means incorporating and integrating the loss into your life. It means assuming a new identity as someone who has experienced the death of someone they love. It means living in the world without your person.

It's understandable that you might not want to accept these changes. You may find it hard to want to live in the world without your person. You may wish for things to go back to the way they used to be. But the longer you resist learning how to be in the world now that they are gone, the longer you will experience turmoil, unease, and anxiety.

To live with your loss, you must:

- Fully acknowledge that the loss has happened and your life will not be the same.

- Build new routines.

- Talk about your loss with supportive people.

- Find ways to honor your person.

- Create and use rituals.

- Acknowledge and honor who you are becoming.

- Seek support as you build a new identity.

- Remind others that you are grieving.

- Cultivate resilience.

- Accept and learn to work with your life changes.

- Be patient and compassionate with yourself.

- Seek meaning.

Reflection

Reflect on the ways in which you feel you have integrated your loss into your life. Examine the ways in which you are resisting or avoiding.

Cultivating Resilience

The concept of resiliency as it relates to grief can feel contradictory. There are many points along your journey when you want nothing to do with rebuilding or embracing your life after loss. The idea can seem downright offensive at times or make you feel as though you are forcing yourself to move on from your person and your grief.

It can feel impossible to imagine ever wanting to be happy again. The idea of thriving in our lives again, of ever being okay without our person, can bring up feelings of guilt and betrayal. Within these experiences, the mere suggestion of resilience can make us feel like we should be moving on. But resilience does not mean you have to let go of your person, and it does not mean you have to stop grieving. Resilience is a tool you use as a means of figuring out how to be here without them. You can always miss them and always wish they were here, *and* you can still live a meaningful life.

There comes a point in the grief journey at which we can make a choice about how we will move forward in our lives, and resilience is part of that.

"What was I going to do? The choices seemed basic and slim:
Die. Exist. Live. I wanted to die, but with two young children to
care for and a husband, that wasn't an option. Exist. I could do
that. I was doing that now. But how flat and lifeless. How dreary
and endless the long march would be until I met Charlotte again.
The only option that resonated with me was to live. But how?
I wanted to want to live. That was the best I could do in that
moment."

—Sukey Forbes, from *The Angel in My Pocket*

Cultivating resiliency after loss is about making the choice to live with loss. Some of us go through so great a loss that we only ever feel that the best we can do is exist. But for others, the search for resiliency is a way of not just surviving the loss but learning how to be present to our lives and how to live in them again *despite* the loss.

It may be necessary to remind yourself over and over that by choosing resiliency, it does not mean you are choosing to let go of your person or even move on from your grief. Resiliency is about finding a balance. It's about allowing ourselves to grieve *and* encouraging ourselves to live at the same time.

Simply put, resiliency is the ability to adapt to challenging circumstances that arise. Resilience is something that all humans are capable of, and it's something we have all relied on at different times and in different capacities throughout our lives.

If a person demonstrates little emotional stress when faced with difficulty, this does not necessarily mean they are resilient. Instead, resilience is embodied *when* we suffer and *when* we fail, yet continue to try, despite those challenges. Just as being brave doesn't mean we're not scared, being resilient doesn't mean you will automatically succeed. Being brave means that you do something even when you're scared, and being resilient means you keep trying even when it's difficult.

It's true that some people are indeed more resilient than others, but it is not a fixed trait. Resilience can be learned, and it is an ability that anyone is capable of cultivating. True resilience is the ability to adapt and grow in the face of adversity, grief, and loss.

THE FOUR THEMES OF RESILIENCE

Resilient Thinking

Resilient thinking means leaning into positive and hopeful thoughts and away from negative and fear-based thoughts.

- I believe in myself.

- I can handle difficult experiences.
- My life has meaning.

Supportive Relationships

Resiliency requires support. Humans are social creatures, and we need to be able to rely on the help of others to move through challenges. We need love and nurturing. Building support is integral to resiliency in grief.

- I will seek and accept help.
- I will build supportive relationships.
- I can rely on my community.

Emotion Management

The intense emotions of grief are new to many of us. It can take work to learn how to manage our emotions in healthy ways.

- Acknowledge your difficult emotions in a nonreactive manner.
- Reach out for support during difficult moments.
- Seek and choose healthy coping mechanisms.

Build on Strengths

We have all utilized resilience at one point or another in our lives. Remind yourself of times when you have overcome hardship in the past, and consider what traits or talents were helpful in doing so.

- Recall times when you have overcome hardship.
- Consider what helped you get through hard times in the past.
- Recognize your unique traits and talents that you can rely on for strength.

WAYS TO BUILD RESILIENCE

Build Connections

- Prioritize and deepen your existing relationships.

- Join a grief group or online grief community.

- Talk about your grief to the people who care about you, and tell them how they can support you.

Practice Self-Care

- Take care of your physical health with diet, exercise, and sleep.

- Practice mindfulness and meditation.

- Avoid unhealthy substances like alcohol and drugs.

Cultivate Resilient Thinking

- Strive for a positive and hopeful outlook.

- Lean toward rational thinking and away from negative/catastrophic thoughts.

- Accept that change is part of life.

Find Purpose

- Find ways to help others.

- Create and move toward large and small goals.

- Seek opportunities for self-discovery and growth.

EXPLORING PAST RESILIENCY

Think about a time in your life that was demanding or difficult. Reflect on how you handled it and what helped you adapt to the changes it brought to your life.

- Describe the challenging time.

- What was your goal?

- What challenges did you have to face?

- Describe the difficult emotions you experienced.

- What personal skills helped you overcome the situation?

- What kind of mindset did you use to face the challenges?

- Did you accept support from the outside?

- How did you cope?

- Based on this past experience, are there resilience techniques you can apply to your current situation?

EMBRACE SOCIAL SUPPORT

Accepting help from friends, family, and community when we are grieving can improve well-being, self-esteem, physical health, and our ability to cope with stress.

- **EMOTIONAL SUPPORT:** Ask for help from people who can help you manage your emotions, show empathy, and listen to you.

- **PRACTICAL SUPPORT:** Seek out people who can help you navigate practical challenges like finances, transportation, and childcare.

- **INFORMATIONAL SUPPORT:** Utilize the people in your life who are good at researching things and providing information, advice, and resources.

- **SOCIAL SUPPORT:** Rely on people who are good at providing love, nurturing, and connectedness in your life.

BUILDING SOCIAL SUPPORT

Some of us don't have large families, lots of friends, or a preexisting community to rely on, but that doesn't mean you can't build these things for yourself.

Strengthen Your Existing Relationships

- Make concerted efforts to stay connected to friends and family.

- Choose to prioritize your important relationships.

- Try reaching out to your wider circle of friends and acquaintances that you may not have relied on before.

Increase Community Interaction

- Participate in clubs.

- Volunteer.

- Get involved in church or other institutions of faith.

Seek Professional Support

- Attend grief support groups.

- Find a therapist.

- Join an online grief community.

CULTIVATING HOPE

It's normal to feel a sense of hopelessness in the face of loss. Sometimes we have to make extra effort to cultivate a sense of hope again. Ask yourself the following questions:

- What does hope mean to me?

- When have I felt most hopeful in my life?

- How have my hopes changed throughout my life?

- How has being hopeful or hopeless influenced the choices I've made in life?

- What gives me hope?

- What needs to happen for me to feel hopeful again?

MAKE A RESILIENCY PLAN

Having goals and making plans is an inherent way of cultivating resilience. For each prompt below, think of two or three ways you could cultivate resiliency.

- Establish routines.

- Build connections.

- Make new friends.

- Take care of my physical health.

- Practice self-care.

- Manage my emotions.

- Feel gratitude.

- Volunteer or support others.

- Seek opportunities for self-discovery and growth.

- Cultivate hope.

- Pursue joy.

- Find purpose.

Reflection
Think about a time in your life that was demanding or difficult.
Reflect on how you handled it and what helped you adapt to the
changes it brought to your life.

Two Things Can Be True

You can wish they weren't gone *and* be glad that you are still here.

You can yearn for them, *and* you can be okay on your own.

You can feel immense sadness about your loss *and* also experience happiness.

You can be angry at them *and* love them.

You can feel afraid *and* also hopeful.

You can feel betrayed, *and* you can miss them.

You can recognize that they hurt you, *and* you can want them back.

You can be full of grief *and* full of laughter.

You can wish this had never happened, *and* you can be grateful for who you have become because it did.

Where Is My Person?

Somewhere along the journey of grief, we are inevitably confronted by questions we may have dismissed previously in our lives. When we lose someone we love, we often spend some amount of time contemplating where they are now. *Are they okay? Can they see me? Are we still connected? Will I ever see them again?*

No matter what beliefs you hold, losing someone close to you usually evokes these kinds of questions. They may be ones you have never considered. But it's normal to ask them. And it's normal to want to know the answers. That's because moving forward and integrating loss into your life is not about letting go of your person. On the contrary, it's about finding ways to maintain a connection to them.

Creating a new relationship with your person is part of grieving consciously. It's part of living with loss, and it's part of accepting your new identity. This relationship does not have to be faith-based, although it can be. It does not have to be spiritual, although it can be. Creating a continuing relationship with your person is as simple as finding ways to feel connected to them. This can be through honoring them or simply living your life in ways that are meaningful to the relationship you had.

This new relationship with your person will not be the same as the one you had when they were here. And creating this new relationship won't necessarily be something you feel ready to do in the beginning of a loss. Sometimes it takes a long time to accept that your former relationship is over and to even want to create a new relationship. And yet for others, this new relationship is something that begins to happen organically after a loss.

For those of us who resist creating a new relationship, it may be a long time before we are ready, and it may require some work. And others of us who have resisted this new relationship may be suddenly catapulted into the throes of it by unexpected circumstances, such as becoming a parent when we have lost a parent or encountering someone in our lives who brings our person back in some way.

What matters is that you open yourself up to the idea that you *can* have a relationship with the person you lost. They can still be part of your life. You can call on them, communicate with them, and commune with them, and in time you will feel more and more comfortable doing so.

The truth is that you will forever carry an internal version of your person with you. As long as you think about them, then you have a relationship with them. You'll be astounded at how that relationship can continue to grow and change. Just wait and see.

Reflection
What are the ways in which you feel connected to your person?
What are ways you can think of to strengthen that relationship?

Contemplations

Who you were before this happened feels farther away now. You may still yearn to be that person, but you know it is no longer possible. Besides, you've come too far. Surrendering was easier than you thought. It feels like relief. It feels like being held instead of trying to hold on.

The path ahead is something you can see more clearly now. That doesn't make it easier, but you feel less awkward stumbling along. You have more clarity, more balance. It's easier to pick yourself up when you fall.

Others are beginning to understand that you have changed as well. Some of them appreciate the you that is emerging, and others are slipping away quietly. You're glad for the paring down. You're seeing what matters more than you once did. And there are so many things that don't really matter, and what does matter shines more brightly.

Your person is emerging here and there, glimpses of promise that they are not gone altogether. It's not what it used to be, not even close, but you are starting to understand that they are still with you.

The path looks different now. More color, more detail, things you hadn't noticed before are catching your eye. You've tried on lots of things along the way—kept some, discarded others—know yet that you'll have to release and try a few more.

But you're still here. You're still breathing. You know that's all you have to do.

PART FOUR

Transforming Through Grief

There is another side to loss. You are starting to feel it. You are not grieving like you were in the beginning. Your grief is not gone, but it is not overtaking you as it once did. Your grief has not been diminished, but you have learned to carry it like a torch as you move through the world. More importantly, you are moving through the world again. But deep inside you know that there is more than just moving through the world. Transformation awaits.

The Other Side of Loss

Grief transforms us. It asks so very much of us. Losing someone we love enables us to see the world in ways we never have before. Grief asks us to unearth the very depths of who we are. And living with loss requires an examination of what really matters. Grief strips us down to our very essence, and if we are to live in the world again, we must rebuild ourselves as whole again.

You are not who you were before you lost your person. You will never again be who you once were. But you know that now, and it is a truth you have accepted. You are becoming familiar with this new version of yourself. Perhaps you even like who you are now, even though the path to getting here is one you never wanted to walk.

> *"You will not get over the loss of a loved one; you will learn to live with it. You will heal and you will rebuild yourself around the loss you have suffered. You will be whole again, but you will never be the same. Nor should you be the same, nor would you want to."*
> —ELISABETH KUBLER-ROSS

Wherever you are right now, your grief is not over. In many ways it will never be over. Your loss will live with you always. But your grief has offered you the profound opportunity to be present to your life. Grief asks us to seek and make meaning of our pain and our tragedies. Grief asks us to seek ways to feel whole again.

You acknowledge that none of this is anything you ever wanted. None of this is something you could have imagined for yourself. And in the beginning of your loss, you did not want to make meaning. You did not want to rebuild. You did not wish to ever be whole again. You did not want to be here without your person. You wanted time to stop, the world to pause.

But it didn't. Time kept marching on, and now you are here.

There is another side to loss. Getting there requires only what is required to be human. The questions we have along the way cannot always be answered in words. The experience of grief cannot be contained within the confines of language. It is something that must be felt and communicated through sensation, emotion, sound, and breath.

Even when we doubt our ability to heal, our bodies never do. Our hearts keep beating. Our lungs continue to yearn for breath. So just breathe. And let yourself transform.

Reflection
What do you know now that you didn't before loss?

Post-Loss Growth

The growth we are capable of experiencing as a direct result of loss is often unexpected. But those who experience it will tell you that it is a strangely beautiful by-product of the pain and hardship they have endured.

There is a growing body of research around the idea of post-traumatic growth, a concept developed in the 1990s by psychologists Richard Tedeschi and Lawrence Calhoun that describes a psychological phenomenon that readily applies to those who have undergone significant hardship and trauma within their experience of loss.

Not everyone experiences this post-traumatic growth. Those who do typically have endured an immense amount of pain and distress with their loss, and the growth that follows does not replace the pain. In fact, the two may continue to coexist—you may continue to carry intense grief yet also feel that you are experiencing a unique and positive transformation.

This kind of growth and transformation is not necessarily achieved by choice. Rather, it is almost only ever achieved by truly being present to your pain. When you allow yourself to feel the magnitude of your suffering and yet continually seek ways to cope and heal, transformation will occur.

It's important to know that the growth you experience is not something that is supposed to feel preferable to the loss you have endured. This means that you do not ever have to feel glad that this trauma occurred, or grateful that your person died so you could experience this transformation. It's more that you can appreciate your growth while still wishing you had never had to go through what you did to achieve it.

Post-loss growth is not an end goal, and again, it is not something that all of us experience in the absence of someone we love. Nonetheless, it is and can be a beautiful part of your terrible experience. Your growth will coexist with your anguish, with your yearning, and with your grief.

Although research suggests that post-traumatic growth is more prevalent than lingering struggles like depression and anxiety, there are some of us who will never feel as though we have gained anything from our loss, and that is okay.

And while there are ways to seek and cultivate transformation after loss, this is different from the concept of cultivating resilience. Whereas resilience refers to the ability to withstand hardship and return to a baseline of functioning, post-loss growth is something that goes beyond a return to "normal"—hence the repeated use of the word *transformation*.

We *transform* through grief when we learn new things about ourselves and the world. We transform when we can reflect on previously held beliefs and assumptions, let go of destructive coping methods, release negative and anxious thoughts, and use our newfound understanding of the world to become someone better than who we were before.

This transformation does not come easily. It requires facing immense pain and sorrow. It requires reflecting on poor choices we've made or behavior that we regret. It requires strength and the willingness to keep trying even when it all feels overwhelming. This transformation also requires support, compassion, and empathy from both ourselves and the world around us.

When we do achieve this kind of growth, the beauty and depth it can add to your life is immense. You may experience

- A greater appreciation for life

- A new sense of what really matters

- A bigger appreciation for small things

- Gratitude for what you have

- Deeper and more intimate relationships

- More compassion and empathy for others

- A heightened ability to receive compassion and empathy from those around you

- The ability to connect with new people

- Better boundaries with harmful or negative people

- A greater appreciation for your close relationships

- An enhanced sense of personal strength and adaptability

- New methods of coping and moving through hardship

- Enhanced feelings of confidence and independence

- An increased openness to possibility and change

- New spiritual beliefs and understanding of the world at large

Perhaps you are already experiencing some of these changes, or maybe you just sense glimmers of them at the far edges of your anguish. Whatever your experience of post-loss growth, remember that this kind of transformation is not supposed to serve as a replacement for your loss and your grief. Remind yourself that two things can be true at once: You can always wish your person were still here, *and* you can feel gratitude for who you have become since losing them.

Reflection
Reflect on all the positive ways you have grown since your loss.

The Long Arc of Loss

It's a paradox. You do not ever want your grief to end, and yet you also cannot fathom how you will live with it for the rest of your life. Accepting that your grief will continue throughout your lifetime can feel both comforting and frightening. But grief changes over time, and the acute grief we feel in the beginning of a loss is not the same grief that we will carry with us over time.

In contemporary understandings of the psychology of grief, there is finally recognition that we grieve throughout our lifetimes. Grief is no longer expected to be tidied up and gotten over after the first year, even though you may still encounter echoes of that sentiment here and there. And when we can acknowledge this for ourselves, we are able to heal and grow *with* our grief, not despite it.

Author and grief expert Hope Edelman explores the long arc of loss in her book *The Aftergrief*, where she carefully outlines the way that our grief changes and the different kinds of grief we experience as the years move forward.

NEW GRIEF: HERE AND NOW

New grief is the raw, immediate grief that comes with your initial loss. It's a feeling that didn't exist before. It is a physical and emotional experience. The emotions are a roiling combination of panic, anguish, sorrow, anxiety, anger, relief, guilt, and hopelessness, among others. This new grief often feels unbearable and impossible to withstand. There are often physical symptoms like sleeplessness, weight loss, and heart palpitations. Brain fog, memory dysfunction, disorganization, and a lack of motivation are common. Our innate coping skills of avoidance and denial surface during this time to give us breaks from this kind of acute grief.

New grief is something that we can feel multiples times as we experience subsequent losses throughout our lives. It doesn't necessarily become easier, but it does become more familiar. And each experience of new grief remains specific and unique to the person we lost, defined by the relationship we had, how our person died, and our current life circumstances and level of support.

When we are experiencing new grief, we may feel that it will never end, but new grief eventually gives way to old grief.

OLD GRIEF: RECURRENT AND RESURGENT

While new grief is a present-day reaction to a recent loss, Hope Edelman defines old grief as "a response in the present to a loss from the past." Old grief is recurrent and unpredictable and sometimes difficult to decipher. When old grief suddenly surfaces after you feel you have been on steady ground for a while, you may feel shaken or even ashamed for thinking you had been doing okay when now you clearly aren't. When old grief surfaces, we may find ourselves—months or even years after our loss—missing or grieving the loss of our person all over again.

Old grief surfaces when a trigger in the present reactivates the thoughts and emotions connected to our loss. We experience this resurgence frequently around dates of remembrance like your person's birthday, Mother's Day, or the anniversary of their death. Old grief also shows up when we experience more loss and find ourselves in another phase of new grief for someone else. Fortunately, these resurgences of old grief are typically temporary and short-lived. However, these flare-ups of old grief can be expected to resurface throughout our lifetime.

CYCLICAL GRIEF

An aspect of old grief, cyclical grief is often tied to calendar dates, such as the date when your person died or became ill, but it can also be evoked by a time of day, a day of the week, or even a season. If your person died on a Tuesday or in the spring, you may feel that cyclical grief on that day of the week or the start of that season.

Cyclical grief most often comes with somatic reactions. You may feel this grief in your body before you are even conscious of what it is connected to. You may feel "off" or disoriented or sad or irritable in the days leading up to a particularly potent date or time without quite realizing why. And when we are conscious of an impending date looming, we often feel anxiety leading up to the day—a feeling that is often worse than the actuality of the day.

This cyclical experience often carries more weight, not less. With each recurring date our cumulative grief builds, bowing under the weight of yet another Mother's Day without our mom, another birthday missed, another holiday gathering in their absence. And as the years go on, we generally find ourselves alone in observing them as the support we received in the beginning has since ebbed. Finding ways to anticipate these dates, to have support in place, and to honor our grief can help immensely.

GRIEF SNEAK ATTACKS

Grief sneak attacks occur when old grief is unexpectedly triggered by something like a song on the radio or a smell associated with our person, or even coming across someone who looks like the person we lost. These kinds of triggers are impossible to anticipate and can instantly evoke acute feelings of sadness and longing.

RESURRECTED GRIEF

Resurrected grief occurs when a new loss in the present reactivates old grief from a past loss. This happens when aspects of a new loss evoke an old loss or when old grief has been suppressed or trauma has not been processed.

Resurrected grief can also occur when we go through a major life change such as moving, career shifts, breakups, and divorces. When grief is resurrected in these instances, we find ourselves grieving the past, the present, and the past *within* the present.

NEW OLD GRIEF: ONE-TIME TRANSITIONS

In the beginning of a loss, we often find ourselves contemplating what it will feel like to move through future life events without our person, but we cannot truly know the grief these events will trigger until we are feeling it in the moment. Even though we can conceive of getting married without our parent there, the grief we feel when we actually walk down the aisle is something new within our old grief.

We also experience new old grief as we mature and cross thresholds from one life phase into another, finding ourselves yearning anew for someone we lost as we experience an aspect of life we wish they were here for. Even during some of our happiest moments and in the midst of great achievements, we may feel waves of sadness and grief that our person is not here to celebrate with us.

New old grief often surfaces during age-related dates, such as turning the age your person was when they died, reaching a death anniversary that marks your person being gone longer than they were alive, or one of your children reaching the age you were when you experienced the loss. These particular dates can become quite significant in our lives—often creating anxiety or serving as motivation for life goals—but they almost always evoke this new old grief.

YOUR AFTERGRIEF

When you are able to understand and accept that there is a long road of grief ahead of you, you can better prepare and process all the old and new grief as it occurs. Acceptance won't make it easier to feel the grief, but it will become something more familiar and less disorienting.

Reflection
Draw a grief timeline of your past grief and future grief.

Your Story of Grief

As humans we are innate storytellers, and the story you tell about your loss is an integral part of your experience of grief. Even if you don't consider yourself a storyteller, you probably have a story you tell about your first car or one about how you met your partner. We are constantly generating stories about the events that occur in our lives, and losing someone we love is one of those events.

However, all stories shift and change over time. They change because memory changes. And they change when we are afforded opportunities to understand certain events in new and relevant ways. Our stories also shift when we process and release feelings of guilt, shame, and fear.

As you move further along your path of grief, you will notice ways in which your story of loss changes. Sometimes these shifts in the narrative occur unexpectedly, and sometimes we ourselves are responsible for the evolution of our story.

In the beginning of a loss, we may focus on details and dates that fade in time, becoming less important or less acutely painful as we are better able to zoom out into a wider view of what happened. And as we resolve feelings of guilt or release anger we have been harboring, the story shifts yet again as other pieces of the story are able to emerge once the focus is removed from the pieces we let go of.

You will also find that as you mature and grow you will inevitably come to understand yourself, your person, and the world at large in ways that also contribute to changes in the story. When you find forgiveness for yourself or others, or when you begin to recognize positive shifts in your identity, you may find yourself telling a story that is different from when it first was written.

Sometimes we may feel reluctant to let go of pieces of the story, even though we have come to realize that they no longer hold weight. When this happens, take a look at how those false truths have served your grief process or helped you cope, as a way to beginning to accept this new version that is emerging.

Remember that, because this story belongs solely to you, and you have the power to reframe the theme of your story or to view your story through a different lens. You also have the power to give voice to parts of the story that may have been silenced or stifled. And you have the right to explore parts of the story that are unclear, yet to be resolved, or have been concealed.

As your grief journey continues to unfold, it is not uncommon to reach a point at which you may find yourself wanting to search for information that you may not have been ready to incorporate in the beginning. We can investigate our stories of loss in many different ways—by searching through old documents or items, interviewing friends and family, or even using spiritual avenues.

The power of narrative within your grief process is one that should be revered, yet constantly examined as you move forward on your journey. Don't hold onto old narratives that no longer fit who you have become and what you now understand about yourself and your loss.

Reflection
What is your story of loss and how has it changed?

Continuing Your Connection

One of the more meaningful experiences of moving farther out from your loss can be a deepened sense of connection to your person. And if you aren't feeling that yet, there are ways to cultivate it.

I want you to understand that it is completely possible to maintain a continued sense of connection with someone who is no longer here. And you do not need to be spiritual or religious in order to achieve this. It is possible to grow, strengthen, and even heal a connection with someone with whom you had a complicated relationship.

The truth is that as long as you are here, none of your relationships are ever truly over. Your connections to the people you have loved and interacted with continue to live on within you. They of course evolve and change over time, because we ourselves grow and change. And we are all capable of cultivating internal relationships with those whom we have been close with, and even those internal relationships have the capacity for growth and transformation.

Some of us never stop feeling connected to our person, and our ability to transition into a more ethereal relationship with them comes naturally. For others, a new sense of relationship with our person is something that occurs later in the grief journey or builds slowly over time. And yet others of us must put in effort to explore and create this new way of feeling connected to our person.

For many of us, the severance of our physical bond with our person may feel so painful that initially we are not able to open ourselves to the idea that we could have any other kind of relationship with them. Closing ourselves off to this idea is a protective mechanism that shields us from more anguish. However, when we attempt to completely close ourselves off to a continued relationship with someone, we can experience a deep sense of incongruence that may lead to anxiety, irritability, and prolonged depression.

Finding ways to stay connected to your person or working to create a new sense of connection with them can be healing and help you immensely on your path to feeling whole again. And this effort to build and strengthen the relationship after your person is gone can happen at any time. Your person could have died many years ago, or last week. There is no wrong time to begin building this sense of connection.

For some of us this connection truly does come naturally. This may be due to various things like your personality, the relationship you had with your person, or your spiritual beliefs. Having and maintaining this sense of connection with your person does not necessarily make your grieving process easier—it does not erase the pain of losing them, and it is almost never preferable to the connection you had with them when they were here in the world—but it can ease that sense of incongruence that others experience when they feel severed completely from their person.

For those of you who are struggling to feel connected to your person, take heart—there is no time limit on when you can work to build or rebuild this connection, and there are many things you can do to cultivate a new relationship and create ways to bring your person into your life again. The relationship will not be what it was when they were here with you, but it will serve to help you feel close to them again and be a means of carrying them forward with you in your life.

For those of us who had a close and connected relationship with our person when they were here in the physical world, it can be incredibly distressing to feel that it is over. You may experience intense sorrow, yearning, anxiety, anger, and depression when you believe that your relationship has ended. Moving out of that mindset requires a willingness to do so, and in order to open up to a new sort of relationship you must also feel a desire to do so. Doing this does not mean that it's okay that they are gone, that you are letting go of what you had, or that it's okay that they died the way they did. Rather it means you are cherishing and honoring them more than ever by being willing to open up to a new way of maintaining your sense of connection to them.

Again, let this come in time. If you do not feel ready to hold your person in your life in a different way, do not assume that you are doing something wrong or that it will never happen; it just means you are grieving as only you know how to do, and this timeline is part of your process.

However, when are you ready to renew, rebuild, or deepen a sense of connection to your person, there are many ways to go about it.

For some of us this new relationship will occur naturally in time. In the beginning of a loss, we may feel more disconnected than ever from our person due to the enormity of our grief. We may yearn to hear their voice in our head, to dream about them, or to see or feel signs that they are still with us, but instead feel none of those things. But often, as our grief softens and as we gradually become more comfortable living with our loss, memories may surface, dreams may become more frequent, and the sense that they are still with us becomes more prevalent.

For others of us, our connection to our person may come in a burst due to something that occurs in our life—becoming a parent may bring an unexpected feeling of closeness, taking on work or service that was part of your person's life may evoke their presence, and sometimes things like turning an age your person was or having an experience that was particular to them may suddenly bring them into your life again.

And yet others may have to strive to create that feeling of connection again. We may have to first overcome feelings of loneliness, resentment, guilt, and fear before we can reach a place where we feel open to the connection. Even when we don't have some of these emotional blocks, we may still have to work to ease open a door to that connection. Easing open that door may look like writing letters to them, taking on a project that was meaningful to them, spending time with people they were close to, or even deepening our spiritual side.

When we lose someone close to us, we may feel that we can no longer converse with them or receive advice or input from them, but those interactions are still possible. When we know someone well or spent many years interacting with them, their thoughts, responses, and even humor become internalized. Try closing your eyes right now and conjuring up your person. Now ask them a question you would have asked them when they were here. Maybe it's about work or your marriage or even if they like the shirt you are wearing. I'm almost sure you know what their answer would be, what tone of voice they would use, and what kind of advice they would give you.

You don't need to know or feel that their words are coming from beyond. That doesn't matter. Because a very real version of them exists within you already. You can begin building or deepening your relationship by continuing to rely on them and continuing to seek their counsel and their love. Close your eyes and talk to them. Ask them what they would tell you right now and listen for their response. Ask them something funny, or something hard, and listen to what they have to say. You can do this any time you feel the urge. And doing so will ease that awful sense of disconnect and will bring them back to you.

Your person lives within you. They are there waiting for you, whenever you are ready.

Reflection
What are all the ways your relationship continues to exist?
What are ways you can enhance this feeling of connection?

Exploring the Afterlife

You are wondering what happens when we die. Grieving consciously means entertaining questions and thoughts in ways you never have before. It's okay to want to try on new beliefs and to feel curious about new religions and philosophies. And it's not uncommon to discard beliefs you've held for as long as you can remember. Questions and doubts and fears may arise. That's okay.

These existential ponderings are a natural part of your healing and growth process. Learning how to be in your life again after loss often means finding a new framework with which to understand the world. And finding ways to stay connected to your person sometimes means that the path to that connection lies behind doors you have yet to push open.

WHERE TO BEGIN?

Start by giving yourself permission to be curious. Don't dismiss the questions as unanswerable or unaskable or awkward. Instead, pause and listen to these questions as they arise within you. Some of them will be ones you've never asked before. Others will be questions you're not sure you should be asking. And some of the questions will feel impossible to answer. None of this means you should ignore or shove away the things you're wondering about.

Start by simply allowing yourself to be curious. Even when fear arises. Even when doubt surfaces. Even when shame or guilt pokes its head through the curtain.

It's normal to feel a little trepidation about letting yourself ponder what happens when we die. This is the stuff that no one talks about.

And that's because the unknowable is the root of all anxiety. For as long as we have existed, humans have feared what is unknowable. Death is nothing but the great unknown. Allowing yourself to face that fear is what will see you through it.

Go slowly. Let it be okay when thoughts surface, and become a gentle observer of it. The thoughts you have about what happens after this life are just thoughts. Creating space for new and reassuring thoughts about the afterlife will help diminish any anxiety you feel.

Death is not something we are in the habit of talking about with the people around us. You may not even know what some of your closest friends and family members believe about the afterlife. But looking into this realm for yourself is part of living with loss and healing your grief.

When you start down this path of opening yourself up to these kinds of existential questions, be patient. Even very simple questions may take you weeks, months, even years to ponder. As you go, let yourself explore books, theories, and philosophies. Pick and choose what resonates for you.

1. WHAT DO YOU THINK HAPPENS WHEN SOMEONE DIES?

Notice your immediate response to this question and think about it for a moment. Is your first answer something you were told and internalized as a child? Is it something your parents worked to instill in you? Does it come from a religion or culture you were raised within?

There is nothing wrong with whatever lies at the foundation of your initial response to this question. All that's important is that you get clear on where it stems from. Now that you are living with loss, the answer to the question of what happens when we die has taken on more meaning. Exploring preexisting beliefs is the way we create a new framework that can hold space for our view of the world after someone we love is gone. When you examine your preexisting or long-held beliefs, ask yourself: Are they ones that bring you comfort? Do they fit with who you are now and what you know your relationship and love for your person to be?

Believing that nothing happens when we die is also a belief you may hold. As with any other belief, there is no right or wrong. But after a loss, questioning and probing into any of your beliefs is part of the process. So ask yourself: Do you *absolutely* believe that? If the answer is still yes, that's okay. However, if you are unsure, then I urge you to open up to the idea that there might be something else and just see how that feels.

2. WHAT SUPPORTS YOUR BELIEF SYSTEM?

Identifying what beliefs you hold offers an opportunity for you to do some exploration in this realm. Check in with yourself about any curiosity you've had about particular religions or philosophies. Visit a church or a temple. Pick up different books that appeal to you and read about various religions or views of the afterlife.

Discard things that don't fit and keep looking until you find something that resonates and appeals to you. Try visiting other churches or spiritual centers, talk to religious advisers, or attend a meditation retreat.

And let yourself think about your loved one's spirituality or religion. Perhaps they held beliefs that would feel comforting for you to incorporate, which could also bring you an even greater sense of connection to them.

3. WHAT WOULD YOU LIKE TO HAPPEN WHEN WE DIE?

Often we carry so many layers of experiences that influence our beliefs that we haven't stepped outside them and let ourselves even consider other possibilities. If it were up to you, what would you most want to happen when we die?

It's a question you may have to sit with for some time, so give yourself room, support, patience, and compassion. Let yourself imagine what it is you would most want to happen when we die. Remove any restrictions that pop up. If the scenario could be absolutely anything you want, what would it be? Use the answer as a way to guide you toward a framework that inspires you and enriches your life.

Reflection

Reflect on the feelings that came up for you in this chapter. Resistance? Curiosity? Relief? Choose one way in which you pursue answers to your questions about the afterlife.

Embracing Ritual

Rituals **allow us to grieve** without language, without logic, and without regard to time. Rituals are a birthright belonging to humans, although we have long since moved past recognition of this truth. But sometimes we seek out wisdom and long-forgotten truths in times of need. Grief is one of those times.

As you move through the wider arc of your grief journey, one of the most powerful ways you can continue to integrate your loss and stay connected to your person is to make use of rituals. Contrary to what you may think, rituals do not make us more sad. Instead they become an outlet for the pain we are carrying and a way to release some of our anguish.

Rituals within grief are instrumental in helping us consciously move forward within grief, yet also stay connected to our person. Because the use of ritual varies so much within different cultures and religions, you may find yourself opening up to ideas in realms you may not have previously explored.

Rituals can range from small, everyday ones like lighting a candle each evening and creating time to intentionally think about your person, to larger, more ceremonial rituals like funerals, remembrances of life, and sitting shiva. And rituals can be especially comforting during holidays and anniversaries.

If rituals have not been a regular part of your life, begin by asking yourself: What does ritual mean to you? What grief-related rituals have you participated in so far that have been meaningful? Let yourself get creative and design your own rituals or pull from ones you've heard about.

Dr. Kenneth Doka, author and grief expert, defines four types of rituals that can be helpful in the grief process:

- **Rituals of continuity** are rituals that enhance the feeling of a continued bond with your person, such as making their favorite meal every month.

- **Rituals of transition** are rituals that mark a change in your grief journey, such as donating your person's belongings or removing your wedding ring.

- **Rituals of affirmation** are rituals that process emotions related to your person by writing them letters or carrying on traditions in their name.

- **Rituals of intensification** are rituals that commemorate anniversaries and mile markers, such as gatherings, cemetery visits, or donations made in their name.

Some of us experience circumstances that prevent us from attending a funeral, memorial, or other service. Or sometimes there simply isn't one, and creating your own ritual can help provide a sense of meaning and honor. These kinds of rituals are designed to help us say goodbye. They are a way of saying farewell, and a way of helping us feel connected to our person.

While there is a full list of ideas in the "Rituals to Rely On" chapter, try designing your own ritual. It could be something you do just once or only on important dates, or something you do regularly as a way of staying connected.

- Choose whether to have friends or loved ones present or to do this privately on your own.

- Choose a location.

- Choose music and candles or other items of meaning.

- Find photos to display or look at.

- Write or think of something you want to say.

- Invite others to contribute their own ideas to this ritual.

- Decide if this ritual will occur regularly, such as during certain times or even annually.

Rituals can serve as torchlights along your path of grief. They are a way to bring awareness to your process, illuminate grief that needs to be addressed, and enhance your sense of connection to your person. Create a ritual for a special occasion or simply when you are missing your person and wanting to feel connected to them. Rituals are here to soothe our souls and help us tap into the parts of our grief that flow beyond the confines of daily living.

Reflection
Design a simple ritual that you can use any time you are feeling disconnected from your grief and your person.

About Honor and Legacy

What does it mean to honor someone? When we honor someone's life after death, we make efforts to recognize and acknowledge the impact they had on the world around them. Sometimes this impact is most obvious through their family, and sometimes the impact is evident in their work or in the effect they had on their community.

In Judaism, the idea of an afterlife is less about a place we go when we die and more about what we have left behind. This kind of afterlife is composed of the legacies and work we do when we are here. It is composed of the good deeds we do during our life, and the values we instill in others. These are the things that continue to exist after we are gone. They are our afterlife.

Let that be comforting to you in terms of your person's afterlife. Without needing any kind of religious framework, you can acknowledge your person's afterlife by bringing to mind all the ways they continue to exist in the here and now, just by examining the ripple effect (however big or small) they had on the world around them. Reflect on their values, what mattered to them, or simply on times they made someone smile. You have the opportunity to continue to uphold and even add to those very qualities and still-existing impacts.

We can honor our loved ones simply by living *for* them. We do not have to do anything great, or make any grand gestures, or even tell anyone how and why we are honoring our person. Honoring them by living is as simple as continuing to move forward in our lives even though we wish they were still here.

When we honor someone who is gone, we are in essence building a legacy in their name. And if according to the belief that we die twice—first when we take our last breath and second when someone speaks our name for the last time—then by creating a legacy in your person's name they will continue to live on for years, decades, or even generations.

WAYS TO HONOR AND BUILD LEGACY

- Live the life they would want for you.

- Embody their values and teach them to others.

- Continue a project they started.

- Donate to a cause or start an organization.

- Create family rituals around your person's favorite things.

- Tell stories about your person to people who never met them.

- Write a book about them.

- Create a legacy book embodying their values and work that can be passed to younger generations.

- Create a grant or scholarship in their name.

- Keep their traditions alive.

- Speak of them often.

Reflection

If you were gone and your person was here, missing you and grieving for you, are there ways in which you would want them to go on living? Are there ways in which they could honor who you were in the world? Are there ways in which you would hope that they might continue to embody values that were important to you or continue work that was meaningful to you?

The Passage of Time

As you move forward, you will notice that the feelings you have around certain times of the year change. Some dates will grow easier to withstand, and others may actually become more difficult to move through.

You may be feeling the added weight of all the accumulated grief you have been carrying year after year celebrating a particular holiday without your person or marking yet another anniversary without them. You may be feeling the grief that arises when memories fade and traditions get replaced.

In the beginning of a loss your person's absence is obvious and palpable, but as time goes on, you become more used to them not being there, and this presents its own kind of grief. And in the beginning of a loss the people around you are more apt to remember that you are grieving and missing your person, but in time that fades as well.

These are some of the saddest parts of moving forward in life with loss, yet this is why it is important to continue to find ways to connect with your person and to honor them—in these ways you get to carry them forward *with* you.

As these years stretch on . . .

• Don't stop speaking their name.

• Uphold their traditions.

• Ask others to share stories about them.

• Light a candle in their honor at a gathering.

- Refer to them as someone's aunt or grandmother even if that person never got to meet them.

- Play music they loved.

- Talk to them in your head and your heart and out loud in a room.

- Carve out time for reflection and ritual when you find yourself around people who did not know your person.

- Lean on your supportive friends who understand why these days are hard.

- Remember that two things can be true at once—you can miss your person and also be present to your meaningful life.

Reflection

Take a moment to feel compassion for all the time you have endured without your person.

Hope and Grace and Forgiveness

Grief threatens to break us down, but we can choose to let it break us open instead. Hope and grace and forgiveness are available to all of us.

As time wears on after someone is gone, the changes you have incurred become more obvious. Some of these changes are positive and some are negative. Take time here and there to reflect on these changes and decide for yourself if they are still serving you.

In the beginning of loss, we often cling to anger and fear and guilt and distrust because those are protective feelings. They keep us from experiencing sadness, vulnerability, and hurt. But sometimes we can get stuck in those places—they become habitual and overly familiar companions to our loss.

So, stop now and then and consider your story of loss—how has it changed? Are there pieces of it you can let go of? Shame you can release? Forgiveness you can bestow? Are you living a life you are comfortable with? Are you living the life your person would want for you?

Just as fear and anger and shame are always available to us, so too are hope and grace and forgiveness. The same effort is required for both.

The swiftest way to a more peaceful existence is through self-compassion. Return to a place of kindness for yourself as often as you can. It will enable you to feel kindness for others.

Try to remember that forgiving someone isn't something you do for them—it's something you do for yourself. It's a way to free yourself from the burden of anger and hurt you are carrying. Why should you be the one suffering so much for their wrongdoing? Forgiving them doesn't mean they are pardoned. It simply means you want to live a life of peace.

And don't forget that it's sometimes harder to forgive ourselves than others. It's more difficult to show compassion to ourselves than someone else. Keep trying again and again if you have to. Painful feelings of doubt and guilt may surface when you express compassion for yourself. Acknowledge those feelings and keep going. You can forgive yourself whether or not you think you deserve it. You can act in loving ways toward yourself even before you feel that love.

Remember that you can always call on your person. Ask them if they would forgive you. It's likely you know the answer. Don't hold onto guilt or anger as a way of holding onto them. There are more peaceful and loving ways to stay close.

You have been living with pain and grief for a long time. You did not ask for it. You did not choose to have this experience. Yet you can choose who you want to be in the world as a result.

Reflection

Are there pieces of you that remain a little stuck? Reflect on the ways in which hope, grace, and forgiveness can free you to move forward.

Meaning Is Yours for the Making

What meaning is there to be found in grief and loss? Why should we even attempt to find meaning?

This is a question only you can answer. And meaning is something only you can seek and find. It may take days or months or many years. You may uncover meaning only to discard it before you find it again. Meaning is yours for the making.

Wherever you are in terms of finding meaning within your loss, know that this is what we are good at. We are storytellers. We are lovers. We are capable of fantastical inventions and impossible creativity. Meaning is the sort of magic that only humans have the tools to create.

Making meaning of your loss does not mean letting go. Making meaning does not mean that it's okay that your person died. It will never be okay that they died. You have the right to miss them and yearn for them all your days. And you also have the power to create a meaningful life in their absence.

"Everything can be taken from a man but one thing: the last of the human freedoms—to choose one's attitude in any given set of circumstances, to choose one's own way."

—VIKTOR FRANKL

Losing a person we love is one of the surest paths to hopelessness. Some of us feel so much anguish, so much loneliness and isolation, and so much fury that the very idea of meaning becomes wiped from our vocabulary. Because what is the meaning of anything if this can happen? And how could life ever feel meaningful again?

Making meaning isn't about finding a reason why your person died. Nor is it about attributing reason to your suffering. Making meaning is about surviving pain and heartbreak. It is about finding a way to be here without your person. Making meaning is about moving forward.

The meaning you find does not have to be directly related to your person. It only has to do with who you have become in their absence. It has to do with the life you are living right now. You are not who you were before they died, and their death has irrevocably changed the way you see the world.

Losing your person has shown you what really matters. And what really matters is something only you can know. But now that you know what matters, what will you do with that knowledge?

You can choose to live a meaningful life.

A meaningful life is one in which you are awake and engaged and conscious in your world and relationships. A meaningful life is one in which you feel like you have purpose and passion and gifts to share with others. A meaningful life is one in which you are in tune with your inner self and at peace with everyone around you.

Only you know what your meaningful life looks like.

Reflection
Reflect on the ways in which loss has made your life more meaningful.

Being of Service

Grief **is one of the most humbling** experiences a human can endure. But within humility we are afforded the ability to understand our true value. And you are so very valuable.

We all have something to offer the world, and one of the most profound ways to create a meaningful life after loss is by finding ways to be of service. So often in grief, the world feels empty. Our sense of purpose is missing. Hope feels elusive. Our passions are dim. Our creativity is muffled. We feel dormant within the person we once were.

But when you cannot find meaning within your own life, you can always find it in others. And you can find value in being of service to someone in need.

Feeling purposeful does not mean trying to be happy or pushing yourself to love your life again. So often those things are robbed of us in grief. Sometimes they are gone altogether and sometimes just temporarily. But what is important for your survival is feeling that you still have something to contribute to the world. Even if you don't feel purposeful in your own life, you can be purposeful in someone else's.

There is always someone in need. And you always have something you can offer. Maybe it's strong arms. Perhaps it's skilled cooking or financial advice. We all need something, and we all have something to offer.

Understand though, that service is not about helping or fixing. Real service cannot occur unless both people are being served. When you offer yourself in service to another, you are receiving meaning and purpose.

ASK YOURSELF . . .

- Who are you now that your person is gone?

- What have you learned?

- What matters to you now?

- What kind of life do you want to live?

- What do you see in others that you did not before?

- What do you need?

- What do you have to offer?

- What knowledge do you have that others don't?

WAYS OF BEING OF SERVICE

- Donate money, time, or material goods.

- Mentor someone.

- Volunteer your time at a school, homeless organization, animal shelter, or elderly community.

- Begin a charity or organization.

- Make service a company mission.

- Offer to babysit.

- Offer to assist someone who is a caregiver.

- Listen to someone who needs to be heard.

- Grocery shop, take out the trash, or rake a lawn for a neighbor.

- Donate blood.

- Offer a workshop in your area of expertise to a low-income community center or battered women's shelter.

- Adopt a pet from a shelter.

- Be an ambassador of grief. Help others along their journeys of loss.

- Do small acts of service throughout your days—hold the door for people, let someone go in front of you at the grocery store, buy someone's coffee in the drive-through line behind you, pay someone a compliment, give someone a smile.

Reflection
Recognize your value and reflect on ways you can be of service in the world.

Embracing Death

You now have an irrevocable awareness of death. Perhaps you thought you understood what death was, but now you understand it in a much greater capacity. For some of us this creates anxiety, while others are fueled by this awareness, using it to pursue life in richer ways. And some of us experience both the anxiety *and* the motivation that this heightened awareness of death presents.

Fear is a natural reaction to death. Losing your person has forced you to face your own mortality. You may worry about losing more people. You may feel afraid of your own death. But don't stop there. Acknowledge your fear and peel up the lid to see what's underneath.

The secret is that what a true awareness of death provides is an awareness of life. Grief and loss and the fact of death really just serve to wake us up to life. And while this experience comes with anguish and uncertainty, it also comes with liberty and freedom.

> *"Tell me what is it you plan to do with your one wild and precious life?"*
> —MARY OLIVER

So, use your newfound awareness of death to help you live the life you most want to live. Cherish your relationships. Seek meaning and purpose. Honor those who are no longer here. Live with grace.

Don't waste this awareness of death on fear. Embrace death. Let it teach you how to live. Work through your fears of death through therapeutic modalities and spiritual counsel. Do some self-inquiry and examine if some of that fear comes from not living a life that is meaningful. Are there changes you want to see happen? Amends you need to make? Plans you need to put in place?

Rather than running from thoughts of your own death, allow yourself to plan and prepare. One of the greatest gifts we can give to our loved ones is preparation for our own death. As you now so painfully know, a person leaves behind a whole realm of physical and emotional belongings. Most people do not have plans in place for when they die and we, the people who are still here, are left to sort through them as best we can.

Most of us delay our plans for end of life, feeling that there is no reason to prepare for it when we are healthy or young. But for those of us experiencing anxiety about death, taking precautions and making preparations can be the very thing to set us at ease. Resisting and delaying preparations for death can result in more anxiety. Facing the end of your life, no matter what stage of life you are in, is a gift to yourself and to the people who love you.

WAYS YOU CAN PREPARE FOR END OF LIFE

- Create a living will or trust.

- Prepare advance directives.

- Obtain life insurance.

- Make your funeral/memorial/burial wishes known.

- Task friends with things you would like taken care of after your death.

- Compile a list of belongings you want people to have.

- Create a document that lists all your bills, accounts, and passwords.

- Organize your legal documents such as birth and marriage certificates.

- Decide what you want to happen to your social media accounts.

- Make a list of people to be notified upon your death.

- Make a list of things you'd like to be destroyed upon your death.

- Write letters that your loved ones can read after you are gone.

- Write down your beliefs about the afterlife for your loved ones.

- Make a list of things you want your loved ones to know about you.

- Make a list of memories or advice you wish to leave behind.

- Write about what you hope to be remembered for.

- Describe the legacy you wish to leave behind.

Let it be okay that working on these tasks brings up emotions. Sadness, fear, nostalgia, and grief will arise. But relief too. Relief for yourself knowing that your plans are in place. And relief and hope that those who are here in your absence will have a path to guide them along their journey of grief.

Reflection
How has your awareness of death changed your values?

An Opportunity

Your journey into grief began with an invitation. And by choosing to grieve consciously you have been presented with an opportunity.

You have lost your person, but now you have the opportunity to live your life in a way that honors them. You have the opportunity to grow from your experience. You have the opportunity to see the world as never before. You have the opportunity to embrace pain and anguish and sorrow as a means of seeking meaning and beauty and peace.

Loss need not destroy you. Our lives are meaningful because they do not last forever. If there were no end, there would be no consequences and nothing would matter. Do the work to heal yourself from trauma that has occurred. Seek support for life changes that have been debilitating. Show yourself compassion for this path you did not choose. Keep your heart open to love and hope and possibility.

Loss has granted you the opportunity to know what really matters. Yes, it's true that loss has also gifted you hardship and futility and sadness, but you feel those things because you had a relationship with someone, and it was meaningful. Your grief is an extension of love. Your sadness reflects a longing for the time you shared. The way you are continuing to live your life honors their absence.

Your person is not gone. They will never be gone.

And your journey of grief is not over. It will never be over. Grief and loss are forever part of your life now and with them come opportunities to be more awake, more in tune, and more at peace with what really matters and who you truly are.

Contemplations

What you know now about grief is what you wish you could have told yourself in the beginning. But you understand that you had to come all this way to know what you know.

What you know is not something you can tell someone in words. What you know is that you have become someone else. Your person is gone and so is who you were when they were here.

You are both new and finding your way along this journey together. Because you are still together.

You meet these days in unexpected places. In the sound of rain on the roof. And a song played in a room you walk through. In the eyes of someone you've just met or known from long ago. You and your person find each other when you least expect it, but you also know where to look.

You carry pain like a lake inside you. You never knew you could fit a lake inside you.

This lake of grief has depths you have yet to explore. And even when it is still and calm, the lake means that they are gone and you are still here. Time never stops. Except now time doesn't mean the same thing it meant before. Time means love and purpose and tiny moments that stretch on for years, and years that fly by like minutes.

You and time are both friends and enemies. You know that when your time here ends, it won't mean what you once thought it did. Because you are still here right now. And there is still a ways to go.

Your Grief Toolkit

There are a great many tools that support the process of grieving. Some may already be familiar to you—tools you have used throughout your life to heal and process. Others may feel foreign. I encourage you to try as many of the following suggestions as you feel comfortable with you. You may be surprised by what enables you to better lean into your grief. After all, you are learning new ways to be in the world and as such, you need new tools.

Why It's Worth Exploring the Five Stages and Other Models

I'm quite certain you've heard of the five stages of grief. I'm also quite certain that you have been given a handful of grief books, and maybe even acquired some on your own dime. People give grief books because they don't know what to say or how to help. And we buy these books for ourselves because we are desperately searching for an understanding of what we are going through.

Wanting to learn more about grief is natural, and doing so is beneficial. Engaging in your grief consciously means making efforts to understand more of what you are going through. And within all the books and information about grief, you will encounter many different models of grief. While they differ, there are valuable pieces within each one that will enable you to better understand your experience.

Creating a framework for grief is helpful in that it provides ways for us to build, grow, measure, and recalibrate within our experience. The four orientations of conscious grieving were born from the years I have spent observing and accompanying the grief of others. Relying on the theory that it is beneficial to lean into grief, rather than avoid or conquer it, I can return to the tenets of conscious grieving as a model to help myself and others move through the process in a way that truly promotes healing.

The models below offer their own frameworks with which to navigate a path forward.

ELISABETH KUBLER-ROSS'S FIVE STAGES OF GRIEF (1960s)

Kubler-Ross was a pioneer in the field of death, dying, and bereavement. She researched, wrote, and spoke about end-of-life matters during a time when very few people were even open to exploring this realm, and her work continues to influence our cultural beliefs about grief to this day.

In the twenty-first century, there has been much debate and criticism of the five stages of grief, but they have continued to remain prevalent, and Kubler-Ross's work remains a foundational component of the ways we understand grief.

The five stages were originally outlined for the dying process, rather than for those who are grieving. Kubler-Ross was working in a hospital in Chicago in the 1960s and began to observe that her terminally ill patients were experiencing a progression of psychological phases as they faced death. While the other doctors around her were busy treating the physical symptoms of these patients, Kubler-Ross was more concerned about their emotional experience of dying and observed that they commonly moved through these five phases.

• Denial

• Anger

• Bargaining

• Depression

• Acceptance

These emotions do, in fact, fit quite well for someone who is facing the end of their life. They move through initial feelings of denial, then often anger at their predicament, and then find themselves bargaining with themselves, their doctors, and higher powers. After that, a certain level of depression sets in, followed by some amount of acceptance about what is happening. At the time that Kubler-Ross introduced these stages, they were revelatory, and she eventually decided to apply them to the grieving process as well. But even Elisabeth herself explained that they are not meant to be a linear formula that could apply to any one experience of grief.

> *"The five stages—denial, anger, bargaining, depression, and*
> *acceptance—are a part of the framework that makes up our*
> *learning to live with the one(s) we lost. They are tools to help*
> *us frame and identify what we may be feeling. But they are not*
> *stops on some linear timeline in grief."*
>
> —ELISABETH KUBLER-ROSS

Some of us never experience denial, and others do not feel anger. Bargaining usually comes in the form of rumination and magical thinking. Depression does not happen to everyone, and acceptance is a mercurial experience that comes and goes throughout our experience of loss. We may experience some of these stages or none at all. We move through them fluidly and can even experience more than one at the same time. Look at them as guideposts for a way to better understand your experience, but do not force yourself to make them fit your experience.

SIGMUND FREUD'S THEORY OF MOURNING (1920s)

Freud was the first to suggest a theory for how people should move through grief. His take suggested that you must first allow yourself to grieve and find ways to express it but then make efforts to emotionally detach yourself from the person you lost.

However, when Sigmund Freud later lost his twenty-six-year-old daughter Sophie, he admitted that the pain and emptiness he felt over this loss would never leave him. He acknowledged that it may weaken over time but there was nothing that would erase it altogether. In fact, nine years after the loss, in a letter to a friend, he wrote that he still hadn't been able to come to terms with the experience. Freud finally came to understand that the bond we have with our loved ones shouldn't be abandoned because it is our way of holding onto them after they are gone.

ERICH LINDEMANN'S GRIEF WORK THEORY (1940s)

Dr. Lindemann was a German American writer, psychiatrist, and grief specialist who built on Freud's work by fusing it with his own research in order to develop three tasks that help process and "recover" from grief. As the author of a paper titled "Symptomatology and Management of Acute Grief," he was particularly interested in post-traumatic stress. The steps he noted are:

• Emancipate from one's bondage to the deceased.

• Readjust to a new environment where the deceased is missing.

• Form new relationships.

The term *grief work* was coined by Dr. Lindemann while he was doing research working with grieving survivors of the 1942 Cocoanut Grove tragedy (a nightclub fire that killed hundreds of people). His research is often cited as some of the earliest that revealed the long-term impact of grief and trauma, and he went on to influence both Elisabeth Kubler-Ross and John Bowlby (see below).

Lindemann was particularly interested in understanding the symptomology of grief. The most common symptoms he noted were:

• **SOMATIC DISTRESS**—difficulty breathing, loss of appetite, exhaustion

• **PREOCCUPATION WITH THE DECEASED**—a fixation on specific images, difficult memories, and also positive reflections of the person who died

• **GUILT**—the perception that the grieving person could have or should have done something to prevent the death

- **HOSTILE REACTIONS**—the expression of irritability and anger toward others

- **LOSS OF PATTERN OF CONDUCT**—changes to regular functioning including restlessness, feelings of meaninglessness, and lack of motivation

JOHN BOWLBY AND COLIN MURRAY PARKES'S FOUR STAGES OF GRIEF (1970s)

John Bowlby was a British psychologist and psychiatrist who pioneered attachment theory, which looks at how our early bonds affect our relationships throughout life. He noted that grief is a normal, adaptive response to loss, given that the "affectional-bond" has been broken. Bowlby and his colleague Colin Murray Parkes broke down this adaptive grief response into four phases of grief:

- **SHOCK AND NUMBNESS**—feeling that the loss isn't real and experiencing somatic distress

- **YEARNING AND SEARCHING**—a longing and searching for the person who is gone as we become aware of the void they have left in our life

- **DESPAIR AND DISORGANIZATION**—an acceptance that life will not be the same, accompanied by feelings of despair and hopelessness

- **REORGANIZATION AND RECOVERY**—the phase of grief in which our day-to-day functioning improves and faith in the future is restored

J. WILLIAM WORDEN'S FOUR TASKS OF MOURNING (1980s)

William Worden, PhD, who is the American author of *Grief Counseling and Grief Therapy*, proposed that there are four tasks of mourning we must complete in the grief process.:

- **ACCEPT THE REALITY OF THE LOSS**—which includes rituals like funerals and memorials, and also beginning to talk about your person in the past tense

- **PROCESS THE PAIN OF GRIEF**—experience a range of feelings from sadness, fear, loneliness, despair, hopelessness, and anger to guilt, blame, shame, and relief

- **ADJUST TO THE WORLD WITHOUT THE DECEASED**—a readjustment that happens over an extended period of time and can require internal emotional adjustments, external life adjustments, and even spiritual adjustments

- **FIND AN ENDURING CONNECTION WITH THE DECEASED WHILE EMBARKING ON A NEW LIFE**—seeking an appropriate, ongoing emotional connection with the person who has died while allowing ourselves to continue living

THERESE RANDO'S SIX RS OF BEREAVEMENT (1980s)

Therese Rando, an American clinical psychologist and the author of *How to Go on Living When Someone Dies*, has published many articles and made many media appearances to talk about her theory of grief, which outlines three phases of mourning that encompass six processes.

Avoidance Phase
- **RECOGNIZE THE LOSS**—acknowledging and understanding the death

Confrontation Phase
- **REACT TO THE SEPARATION**—experiencing the pain and emotional responses to the loss

- **RECOLLECT AND REEXPERIENCE THE DECEASED**—reviewing and remembering the deceased

- **RELINQUISH OLD ATTACHMENT**—relinquishing the world in which you were accustomed to living with your loved one

Accommodation Phase

- **READJUST TO A NEW WORLD**—moving adaptively into your new world without forgetting your old one

- **REINVEST EMOTION ENERGY**—investing emotional energy in new people and goals

SIMON RUBIN'S TWO TRACKS OF BEREAVEMENT (1990s)

Simon Rubin is the director for the International Center for the Study of Loss, Bereavement and Human Resilience at University of Haifa in Israel. His two-track bereavement theory outlines an interactive process that is experienced within two realms. The first realm is an individual's bio-psycho-social functioning (physical symptoms, anxiety, depression, relationships, and self-worth). The second realm is the grieving person's relationship with the person they lost (including emotional closeness, conflict, and preoccupation with their death). The two-track theory implies that to assess and cope with their grief, the person needs to attend to both tracks of the process.

STROEBE AND SCHUT'S DUAL PROCESS MODEL OF GRIEF (1990s)

The dual process model of coping with grief was developed by Margaret Stroebe and Henk Schut, who are both professors and clinicians in the field of grief. They studied grief in their work called "The Dual Process Model of Coping with Bereavement: A Decade On." Their theory is that grief operates in two different ways—loss-oriented and restoration-oriented—and that people must oscillate, or switch back and forth, between them as they grieve.

- **LOSS-ORIENTED**—stressors that make you think about your loved one and their death and induce thoughts, feelings, actions, and events that cause you to focus on your grief and pain. For instance, the experience of looking at photos of your person and feelings emotions like sadness, loneliness, and anger.

- **RESTORATION-ORIENTED**—stressors that distract from grief and turn your focus toward daily life and away from feelings of grief and pain. These include work, chores, exercise, and social activities. Stroebe and Schut believe that indulging in these distractions is a healthy way of coping with grief, and that without this behavior the grieving person would be unable to function in their day-to-day life.

- **OSCILLATION** refers to the way that a grieving person moves back and forth between the loss-oriented and restoration-oriented modes of being. Stroebe and Schut encourage embracing the oscillation as a way of emotionally processing and moving forward after loss.

KLASS, SILVERMAN, AND NICKMAN'S CONTINUING BONDS THEORY (1990s)

The continuing bonds concept was first introduced in a book published in 1996 titled *Continuing Bonds: New Understandings of Grief (Death Education, Aging, and Healthcare)*. Authors and grief experts Phyllis Silverman, Dennis Klass, and Steven Nickman questioned prior theories of grief, dismissing ideas that grieving people should "move on" or "let go," and instead presented the case for a new interpretation that includes helping grievers forge an ongoing sense of connection with those they have loved and lost.

Continuing bonds theory focuses on the following tenets:

- There does not have to be an end to grief. When we lose someone we love, we should not feel that we need to "get over" the loss or "move on" from our relationship with the person we loved.

- It's normal to stay connected with deceased loved ones; in fact, we do not ever fully detach from them but instead find new ways to stay connected.

- Our grief-related behaviors are normal. Talking to deceased loved ones, cherishing their belongings, dreaming about them, and hearing their voices are not pathological responses to grief. Rather they are normal coping mechanisms that enable us to adjust to our lives post-loss.

CONSCIOUS GRIEVING (2020s)

Conscious grieving relies on the theory that it is beneficial to lean into grief, rather than to treat it as a malady or an affliction that must be remedied. This model makes the assumption that grieving is a natural process and that all humans have the ability to grieve and the inherent knowledge of how to do so.

The Four Orientations of Conscious Grieving

- **ENTERING INTO GRIEF** invites the griever to allow for an awareness of their initial feelings of grief, even when those feelings encompass denial, overwhelm, and anxiety.

- **ENGAGING WITH GRIEF** encourages the griever to stay present to their grief at a time when their instinct may be to avoid the feelings like guilt, depression, anger, and shame that occur when navigating the complicated realms of holidays and anniversaries, family and culture, and multiple losses.

- **SURRENDERING TO GRIEF** asks the griever to rely on spirituality, self-compassion, and resilience as a way to surrender to the changes in identity that occur within the face of loss.

- **TRANSFORMING THROUGH GRIEF** explores ritual, honor, hope, humility, and grace to invite the griever to consider the opportunities within loss to allow for transformation and meaning.

Again, take what works from these models. Do not feel that you must fit your personal experience into any one of these theories. Use the parts that resonate to enable you to better understand and lean into your loss.

Meeting Yourself in Grief

When we experience a loss, all of who we are rises to the experience. Our personalities, our faults and flaws, our tendencies, and our natural ways of being in the world are asked to meet the demands of this process.

While it is true that grief can change our personalities, altering our thoughts and behaviors, more often than not we find ourselves responding to grief in the same ways that we process and react to any big life changes and emotional experiences. If we are internal and introverted, we grieve more internally and quietly. If we are communicative and outgoing, we are likely to express our grief outwardly through communication, creativity, and connection.

Grief does have the capacity to change us, and sometimes these changes are temporary and sometimes they are permanent. The depths and consistency of the changes depend on the profundity of our loss, our coping abilities, our support systems, and our general outlook on life. Many people feel that they no longer recognize themselves in the face of loss, so vast are the internal and external changes occurring in their lives. In this case, it's important to distinguish our typical responses to grief from personality shifts that may be occurring. Sometimes what might feel like a major change is really just a temporary response to grief. For instance, you may be an extrovert who finds yourself withdrawing from social situations after a loss, but this does not necessarily mean that you have permanently become an introvert.

What you will notice is that some of the long-term personality shifts can be both positive and negative. For example, you may find yourself altered from an optimistic person to a more pessimistic person, or you may find less enjoyment in pleasurable activities and moments than you once did. On the other hand, you may find yourself living more freely and openly now that you recognize how fleeting life is, and things that once seemed overwhelming or tedious may become unimportant in a way that opens you up to heightened experiences of the world.

When we are grieving consciously, the process can become a powerful opportunity to embrace your personality, to lean into its strengths and explore its limitations. In the descriptions below you may find yourself wholly defined within one or spread out through many. Notice that within so many variations of grieving there is not one that reigns supreme above the others. Rather each type works with the personality of the person grieving to help them integrate their loss.

INTUITIVE AND INSTRUMENTAL

Coined by researchers Kenneth Doka and Terry Martin, these two styles of grieving are described as extremes on a continuum. Intuitive grievers experience grief as very intense waves of emotion. Their feelings are felt strongly and expressed as such. Intuitive grievers are inclined to intentionally work through their feelings by talking about them, seeing therapists, and joining support groups. Instrumental grievers tend to process their loss in more cognitive and physical ways and are typically less feeling-based. There is an emphasis on problem-solving as a way of adapting to the new normal of life after loss. Neither style of grieving—instrumental or intuitive—is superior, and many people lean into a blend of both.

INTROVERTED AND EXTROVERTED

Introverts are easily overwhelmed by all that comes in the early phases of grief. Funerals, memorials, shivas, and other gatherings surrounding their person can leave them feeling drained and needing alone time in order to reflect and process. On the other hand, extroverts find them-selves gravitating toward people as they grieve, joining support groups, seeing therapists, or engaging in online communities as a way to seek emotional support and others with whom to process their experience. Neither way is more effective than the other. Instead, what is evident is that embracing your natural inclination and way of being in the world becomes a way of allowing you to lean into your grief.

DISSONANT

Dissonant grievers are those who undergo a conflict between the way they experience grief internally and the way they express it outwardly. This can create a persistent feeling of discomfort and lack of harmony. Some of this dissonance may stem from cultural and familial expectations and traditions. If you are experiencing this dissonance, you may feel caught between what you really feel as you grieve and the image you are required to project to the world around you. Finding ways to stay true to your process and surrounding yourself with those who allow you to grieve the way you need to will ease some of this tension.

OPTIMISTIC AND PESSIMISTIC

These two different outlooks on life create a lens through which we internalize our story of loss. Those of us who lean toward a pessimistic view of the world are more likely to blame ourselves when difficult things happen. We tend to believe the impact of the loss will last forever and to feel that everything we do will be detrimentally affected by this event. After a loss, we may find it more challenging to feel hopeful, and we may need to find more focused ways of coping. For those of us who have a more optimistic view of life, we tend to believe that difficult things happen by chance and that the effects will not be permanent. It is easier for us to remain hopeful that we will be able to move through the experience of loss in way that enables us to continue living our lives in the ways we've envisioned.

DR. SUSAN BERGER'S FIVE GRIEF PERSONALITIES

In her book, *The Five Ways We Grieve*, Dr. Susan Berger outlined five patterns she observed in grieving people as they find their way from their old identity to a new one. Each personality is one we may inhabit in many different ways throughout our process.

The Nomad

Nomads are described as having a wide range of emotions such as denial, anger, anxiety, and confusion. As nomads we may struggle to understand how the loss has affected our life, and our challenge will be to find an identity that aligns with a perspective and purpose that promotes healing. Many of us may recognize ourselves as nomads in the early stages of the grief process.

The Memorialist

Memorialists are those of us who are committed to preserving the memory of our person. We tend to create rituals, memorials, and traditions that help us honor our loved one. All of these activities can help us maintain a sense of connection to our loved one as we move forward.

The Normalizer

Normalizers focus on friends, family, and community and seek to improve and reinvest in relationships following a loss. Doing this can bring us a sense of connection and relieve feelings of isolation and loneliness. Strengthening and improving relationships comes from the new awareness that life can be fleeting and we do not wish to leave anything unfinished.

The Activist

Activists cope with loss by using it to find meaning. We pursue activities and goals that enable us to help others or raise awareness for the way that our loved one died. While these can be noble pursuits, activists must also remember to take time to process their internal feelings of grief when they find themselves overly focused on the external activities surrounding it.

The Seeker

Seekers tend to lean into philosophical and spiritual guidance to find comfort and healing. We look for new ways to understand the world and to find meaning, and for frameworks that can explain our experience of loss. Seekers may find great comfort and stability in religion, spirituality, and explorations of the afterlife.

FEMININE AND MASCULINE GRIEF

Because we are a gender-oriented society, grief is often viewed through feminine and masculine lenses. Our culture places different expectations on different genders, forcing us to fit ourselves into roles that sometimes cause feelings of dissonance.

Feminine grievers are thought of as more intuitive and extroverted while masculine grievers are expected to behave in ways that are more introverted and instrumental. A masculine person is often expected to remain rational, in control of their feelings, and focus on goal-oriented activities. A feminine person is encouraged to express their feelings and seek social support, and is given more permission and more time to move through their process.

These are cultural and social norms that no one should feel obligated to adhere to. No matter your gender, your grief process is unique and must be felt and expressed in ways that only you understand.

Allow yourself to utilize and embrace your unique personality as a means of leaning into your natural abilities to heal and cope. Seek and surround yourself with those who support the style of grief that feels right to you, and protect yourself from those who wish to mold you into a way of grieving that does not feel true to who you are.

Tools for Grief

Loss is something that happens to us, but how we grieve is up to us. Grieving consciously means choosing to intentionally engage with the emotions of pain, sorrow, anxiety, and anger. Sometimes this is easier said than done, as the emotions that accompany loss can be overwhelming and disorienting.

However, there are many useful tools and techniques to support ourselves through grief. Throughout this book you will find mentions of them across various pages. To make it easy, I've outlined all the tools here so that you can return to this section any time you need clarification or understanding.

THERAPY AND COUNSELING

Talking to a skilled professional who is safe and unbiased can serve to both unburden and process all that you are carrying. There are many different types of professional support, and some are more accessible and useful than others. For an in-depth understanding of grief therapy and how and where to find the right therapist, see the chapter in Part Three on "Navigating Professional Grief Support."

EMDR

Eye Movement Desensitization and Reprocessing (EMDR) is a treatment designed to alleviate distress associated with traumatic memories and grief. This method of psychotherapy is very popular for grief as it allows for the ability to reprocess difficult experiences and reduce the physiological response, meaning that it will lessen overwhelming and painful associations you may have incurred around your loss. EMDR is a technique that must be administered by a trained therapist and only requires a few sessions.

CBT

Cognitive Behavioral Therapy (CBT) focuses on changing automatic negative thoughts that contribute to and worsen emotions like depression and anxiety. This treatment is offered by therapists who have been trained in CBT and gives us a way to identify and change destructive thought patterns that influence our emotional state. This is an excellent way to better manage anxiety, rumination, or catastrophic thinking following a loss.

SOMATIC THERAPY

The philosophy of somatic therapy is one that explores how what happens in your life is stored not only in your mind but also in your body. Therapists trained in this technique help you focus on the physical sensations in your body during a discussion of your grief for a more integrated approach to processing loss. Somatic therapy techniques often include breathwork, yoga, body awareness, grounding and centering work, and self-soothing touch.

JOURNALING

This is a practice that will help you find the words for your grief. Keeping a journal also serves to release and unburden difficult emotions and relieve stress and anxiety. It can be a place to store memories you are afraid of forgetting, and a grief journal can eventually become a way to reflect on your path. My recommendation is to set aside five to ten minutes a day to write—doing this before the start of your day or at the end of it will help you reconnect to your grief outside of obligations that require other focus. While you will find many journal prompts throughout this book, you may also choose to simply free-write your daily thoughts or use one of the many grief journals available online.

MEDITATION

Meditation is a practice I recommend more than any other. It is simple, easy, accessible, and provides immediate and ongoing relief from anxiety and overwhelm. This practice calms our nervous systems, resets our thought patterns, and gives us the ability to find space within ourselves and our grief process. Meditation can be done one to three times a day, and there are many books, classes, and apps that can help bolster your practice.

MINDFULNESS

This is also a practice that provides relief from the crush of grief. Mindfulness is simply a way to bring your awareness to the present moment and can be done with many sensory activities like intentional breathing, eating, and walking. After a loss we tend to spend a lot of time in the past or the future, but the practice of mindfulness invites us into the present moment to survey our internal landscape with compassion and curiosity. Like meditation, there are many books, classes, and apps that can help support your practice.

YOGA

This practice incorporates both meditation and mindfulness into a physical experience using a series of stretches and sequenced movements that soothe your nervous system and calm your mind. Yoga is a wonderful way to inhabit your body, get centered, and find compassion for yourself when you are grieving. There are many books, classes, and apps that can help support your practice, and even many offerings designed specifically for grief.

BREATHING EXERCISES

Simple yet profoundly soothing, breathing exercises are an important part of conscious grieving. They allow you to get centered, calm your nervous system when you are anxious or scared, and bring awareness to your present experience. Although there are many different kinds of breathing exercises, these three are a good place to start. Additionally, you may want to consider taking a breathing workshop, downloading a breathing app, or reading a book about breathwork.

- **FIVE-COUNT BREATHING:** Take a deep breath in while you count to five or ten. Then slowly release that same breath to the count of five to ten. This kind of evenly controlled breath helps to get oxygen flowing into your brain, while the counting helps shift the focus of your thoughts away from panic and fear.

- **BOX BREATHING:** Breathe in evenly through your nose as you slowly count to four in your head. Then hold your breath for a count of four. Next, exhale for another count of four. Hold your breath again for a count of four. Repeat for three or four rounds.

- **DIAPHRAGMATIC BREATHING:** Lie on your back with your knees bent. Place one hand on your upper chest and the other on your belly, just below your rib cage. Breathe in slowly through your nose, letting the air in deeply toward your lower belly. The hand on your chest should stay still while the one on your belly should rise. Tighten your abdominal muscles and let them collapse inward as you exhale. The hand on your belly should move down to its original position. Repeat for several rounds.

PHYSICAL CARE

While you will find a more thorough depiction of the physicality of grief in Part One (including more ways to care for yourself while you are grieving), you will note many references to physical care throughout this book. That's because tending to your body in grief is often an afterthought for most of us, yet it is the very thing that helps us regulate and manage the intense emotions brought on by loss.

- **EXERCISE:** Taking walks or doing some form of cardio can help calm your nervous system and induce helpful endorphins.

- **REST AND SLEEP:** These are vital and will help you regulate your emotions.

- **NUTRITION:** Making sure your body is getting enough nutrients will also help ease feelings of irritability and exhaustion. Many people who are grieving experience a loss of appetite. You can try even just drinking smoothies or protein shakes to fuel your body. Again, this will help you withstand the intense emotions you are experiencing.

- **VITAMINS AND SUPPLEMENTS:** Bolstering your immune system during this time is important.

- **HYDRATION:** Water and hydration are important to your bodily functions and can help you feel more balanced.

- **AVOID ALCOHOL AND DRUGS:** These are easy coping mechanisms to turn to when you are grieving, but they can exacerbate anxiety, sadness, depression, and irritability.

How to Ask for Help

After a loss, you will find that many people will say, "Let me know what you need." And while that's nice to hear, in the throes of grief it's sometimes hard to know what you need. But the truth is that we could also use help when we are grieving, whether it's emotional, practical, or logistical support.

Throughout this book, you will notice that I frequently encourage you to seek support and ask for help. Grieving is an immense experience, one in which we cannot always rely on ourselves alone to accomplish. When we grieve in isolation, we risk venturing into dangerous territory such as avoidance, fear, and overwhelm. Finding people who can support you is vital and will serve to enable you to better lean into your grief.

But while no one should be expected to grieve alone, many of us still struggle to ask for help. However, recognizing and acknowledging vulnerability in the face of loss is part of conscious grieving, and you are likely to find that most people are more than willing to provide support and assistance of all kinds.

PERSONAL HELP

- Childcare
- Pet care
- Meals
- Assisting out-of-town guests
- Funeral and memorial planning

HOUSEHOLD HELP

- Housekeeping
- Laundry
- Grocery shopping
- Organizing a loved one's belongings

FINANCIAL HELP

- Funeral and memorial expenses
- Medical expenses
- Collecting benefits
- Settling the estate
- Financial planning

EMOTIONAL HELP

- Guidance around big decisions
- Someone to keep you company
- Someone to talk to
- Someone who can listen

HOW TO ASK

Once you've identified what you need help with, ask your loved ones and community for support. Consider appointing someone you trust to oversee the areas you need help with by having them reach out on your behalf, or even letting them create an online registry or donation account and a schedule for meals and child and pet care.

Any time you feel insecure, reverse the situation and try to imagine how you might feel if someone in your position asked you for help. It's likely that you would feel happy to help, and find it helpful to have specific tasks to assist them with.

Rituals to Rely On

For as long as humans have existed, we have relied on rituals to help us process grief and honor the people we have lost. Rituals serve to help us feel connected with our person, to feel our grief witnessed, and to transform our pain into something physical and even beautiful.

While rituals are deeply personal and you may wish to design your own (see "Embracing Ritual" in Part Four), here are some simple ideas you can also use:

- Light a candle at a certain time each day and think of your person.
- Visit their grave or other memorial location.
- Watch videos or go through photos of your person.
- Travel to a place that was meaningful to your person.
- Travel to a place your person always wanted to visit.
- Write letters to your person.
- Write a story or poem about your person.
- Make your person's favorite meal.
- Enjoy a meal at your person's favorite restaurant.
- Listen to your person's favorite music or songs.
- Watch your person's favorite movie or show.
- Release butterflies or balloons.
- Create art that relates to your person or your grief.
- Create a memory book of your person.

- Throw flowers into a body of water such as an ocean, lake, or river.

- Collect items that were meaningful to your person.

- Give yourself a gift from your person.

- Create an altar for your person.

- Carry a special item of your person's.

- Wear something belonging to your person.

- Host a family memory evening in which everyone brings a memory to share.

- Plant a tree or memorial garden.

- Donate to a cause that was important to your person.

- Perform acts of service in their honor.

- Create a scholarship in your person's name.

- Create a nonprofit in your person's name.

- Purchase a book in your person's name and donate it to a school or library.

- Share your person's favorite recipes with friends and family.

- Name someone after your person.

- Design a shrine or create an altar.

Recommended Reading

Bearing the Unbearable by Dr. Joanne Cacciatore and Jeffrey Rubin

Finding the Words by Colin Campbell

It's Ok That You're Not Ok by Megan Devine

When Someone Dies: A Children's Mindful How-To Guide on Grief and Loss by Andrea Dorn

The Aftergrief by Hope Edelman

Finding Meaning: The Sixth Stage of Grief by David Kessler

The Beauty of What Remains by Rabbi Steve Leder

The Beginner's Guide to the End by Dr. BJ Miller and Shoshana Berger

The Grieving Brain by Mary Frances O'Connor and Callie Beaulieu

What's Your Grief? by Litsa Williams and Eleanor Haley

Acknowledgments

An astrologer once told me that according to the position of the planets when I was born, my particular purpose in this lifetime is guided by two realms: the realm of death and the realm of communication. When I told him that I write books about grief and end of life, he nodded and told me that makes perfect sense. So, in many ways, this book feels like an alignment of my soul. While all my books are about grief and death—each one building upon the previous—I have been working toward *this* book all my life. These pages are born out of a lifetime of grieving because as humans we are always grieving. This is the book I wish I could give my younger self when I felt so broken and alone. But I also know that this book would not be possible without the years of work I have spent exploring ways to heal my own grief and helping others along their diverse paths of loss.

I'm incredibly grateful to those who make books like this possible: my ineffable agent Wendy Sherman, who has championed my work for over a decade. My wise and impeccable editor Maisie Tivnan and everyone at Workman Publishing who worked so hard to make this book beautiful. To all my beloved colleagues who work in the realm of grief—I am so appreciative of your compassion, knowledge, and persistence in giving our culture permission to grieve: Hope Edelman, David Kessler, Rabbi Steve Leder, Allison Gilbert, Meghan Riordan Jarvis, Alua Arthur, BJ Miller, Jacqueline Bush, Shoshana Ungerleider, Tembi Locke, and Angela Schellenberg. I am also deeply grateful to my dear friends who have never failed to show up with love, laughter, and support when I am overwhelmed and drained, and even when I'm not: Jennifer Mack, Caeli Woflson Widger, Catherine Schram, Tarsha Benevento, and Kelle Hampton. Lastly, to my family—my husband Mark, my stepkids Dylan, Willow, and Kirvin, and my children Vera, Juliette, and Everett for putting up with having a writer who talks about death for a mom and partner.

Index